DATE DUE

1-8-00			
DEC 1 2 2000			
GAYLORD			PRINTED IN U.S.A.

Chemicals for the Mind

Chemicals for the Mind

Psychopharmacology and Human Consciousness

Ernest Keen

 PRAEGER

Westport, Connecticut
London

Library of Congress Cataloging-in-Publication Data

Keen, Ernest, 1937–
    Chemicals for the mind: psychopharmacology and human
consciousness / Ernest Keen.
        p.   cm.
    Includes bibliographical references and index.
    ISBN 0-275-96775-1 (alk. paper)
    1. Pyschopharmacology.   2. Consciousness.   3. Altered states of consciousness.
I. Title.
RM315.K44 2000
615'.78—dc21   99-16058

British Library Cataloguing in Publication Data is available.

Library of Congress Catalog Card Number: 99-16058
ISBN: 0-275-96775-1

First published in 2000

Praeger Publishers, 88 Post Road West, Westport, CT 06881
An imprint of Greenwood Publishing Group, Inc.
www.praeger.com

Printed in the United States of America

The paper used in this book complies with the
Permanent Paper Standard issued by the National
Information Standards Organization (Z39.48-1984).

10 9 8 7 6 5 4 3 2 1

Copyright Acknowledgement

Some material in chapter 7 appeared previously in Keen, E., (1988) *Drugs, Therapy,
and Professional Power: Problems and Pills.* Westport, CT: Praeger Publishers, an
imprint of Greenwood Publishing Group.

To Andrew and Whitney—
Cyber-Percussionists Both

Contents

Preface

For the past several years, I have been fascinated by the topic of psychopharmacology—the practice of treating individuals' feelings, those that make them ill (can they be called ill-feelings?), with pills containing chemicals that apparently change certain events in the brain. I have found that not many people outside professional circles want to discuss psychopharmacology. I am not sure why.

Some do not want to talk about psychopharmacology because they are currently experiencing it, either under the care of a physician or a bartender, and in either case they seem to know what they need to know—what the chemical does for them, or to them, personally. Perhaps others recognize a certain uncomfortable similarity between psychopharmacological treatment and simply imbibing mind-altering chemicals.

It is indeed disquieting to let the complexities of alcoholism and the drug war complicate a convenient understanding that Prozac is "treatment" and marijuana is "crime." I appreciate this discomfort, because being uncomfortable suggests a marginal awareness that something is awry, or perhaps even that the root question facing modern individuals, in a psychopharmacologically incontinent society like our own, is a moral question. I have come to believe that the moral dimension of the science of psychopharmacology is what makes me, and perhaps most people, uncomfortable. Furthermore, it has only slowly dawned on me that the moral issues in psychopharmacology are urgent.

From some angles, psychopharmacology is quite a questionable enterprise, from others quite humane, and from yet others quite inevitable. I see it in all three ways. I speak of the morally questionable aspects and the morally humane aspects, but it is the inevitable aspects that should most urgently command attention. Despite the discomforts I noted with the topic, there is a relentless energy in the advancement of this science and this practice, as if it satisfied more than medical motives. The energy is perhaps itself scientific, but also perhaps personal to some people, corporate to some corporations, professional to some professions, and cultural to some aspects of our culture.

Perhaps psychopharmacology is no more of a moral science than psychology and psychiatry have always been. Perhaps drugs have simply made this awareness inescapable. Perhaps they have brought the moral content of the treatment professions out from behind the mask of science. Of course, to change anyone's feelings or thoughts is a moral act. It is always a moral choice when someone intervenes, as is done every day, into the mental life of another in an effort to change that person. When it is done as *therapy*, trying to *heal* an illness, the moral content is made no less by the science from which it comes.

And, yet, there is something new in drug therapy as well, and that is the technological ability to shape one's mind and being. Persuasion and talk therapy are weak indeed compared to the manipulation of minds with pills. There is enormous power here, with implications that outstrip one's current vision. I focus here on the question of the moral implications of the increasing technological ability to change minds. I am barely able to see the question, let alone the answer, but maybe this beginning can provoke a more concerted effort, for it is increasingly dawning on me that the avoidance of these questions creates a kind of violence.

Technology morally unchecked may always become violent, perhaps, so here again this may be familiar ground. But again, the technology of changing minds is not simply like the technology of mastering "nature." We think of nature as an object—a living, vital object perhaps, but the idea of nature is rarely applied to the interior of one's own personal consciousness. That interior is where individuals see and understand; it is mental life, not usually reducible to the terms of nature. One's efforts to so reduce it all fail intellectually, even while they seem to succeed practically. And yet making that effort leads to an even greater failure, which I call *violence*. This is a strong word. Perhaps it should be said that here one glimpses tragedy, the tragedy embedded in the inevitability of, combined with the insufficiency of, dualism.

Acknowledgments

I mention here my most important mentors on the topics of this book: Peter Breggin (1991), Joseph Fell, David Healy (1997), Arthur Kleinman (1988), Theodore Sarbin, Calvin Schrag (1997), and Douglas Sturm (1998).

Introduction

This book focuses on questions too rarely asked by prescribers and receivers of psychoactive drugs: How can it be that problems in one's life, and in one's consciousness, are made better by altering the chemistry of one's brain? An individual's consciousness is a mental reality that is nonphysical. It occupies no space, nor does it share other crucial features of physical reality. And yet mind-altering chemicals, clearly physical agents, have become a staple of mental treatment at the end of the 20th century.

This practice involves theoretical puzzles as old (at least) as Descartes, but the modern results are practical, not philosophical. If a man's problems with his wife or his job make him anxious or depressed, he can get relief from pills. The problems between a person and the world may seem to improve, but they may also fester, unattended in the newfound freedom from sectors of the person's own consciousness. Most doctors and patients believe, however, that "medication" is the treatment of choice for mental troubles as fully as for physical ones.[1]

It is impossible to know how often psychopharmacological treatments actually work *against* solving personal problems, but the dramatic increases and current frequency of such drug practice are well known. As recently as the 1970s and 1980s, chemical treatments were much less common among the general population. In 1997, the antidepressant Prozac drew the second largest expenditure from the U.S. public of all prescription drugs, outsold only by Prilosec, an ulcer medicine. Zoloft and Paxil, drugs very similar to Prozac, rank sixth and seventh in the top 10.

Receivers of these medications obviously find them useful in dealing with depression, compulsions, and obsessions. Children also are increasingly using psychopharmacological agents. A dynamic typical of industry and marketing is clear here. Have these institutional patterns usurped medical ones?[2] Even more challenging, however, is the possibility that the problems addressed with many psychoactive drugs are not medical problems at all. What are called mental *symptoms* are reactions to, or parts of, personal and interpersonal struggles that should be dealt with as normal parts of life, not as diseases.[3]

We do not know, beyond very general terms, how these drugs work in the brain. The same was once true of aspirin, of course. But unlike aspirin, these drugs address not physical pain but mental pain.[4] Behind this difference lies a complex theoretical problem that is unresolved, and more importantly, unacknowledged, in Western medicine. Philosophical dualism is rarely addressed among those who prescribe psychoactive drugs, but they practice dualism with the pragmatic abandon they pursue only at the neglect of very concrete human problems. Drugs that change consciousness may impoverish human experience.[5]

However philosophical the roots of the theoretical problems are, the results are eminently practical. And, however practical the outcomes are, the roots of the problem are eminently philosophical.

In the first chapter, I reveal how the unresolved philosophical problem of dualism has led to two incommensurate ways of understanding everyday life. One language leads into a world of ideas and free will that individuals grasp morally, and the other language leads into a world of things and their mechanical patterns that are grasped causally. Each language shapes the contours of the world in its own way. The world of choices is a moral one; the world of causes is a mechanical one.[6]

Much of "the" world can be seen either way. In family life, and other practical contexts, individuals find themselves using sometimes one language, and sometimes the other, often moving back and forth between these two languages automatically, getting through a day.

But some contexts, such as the psychiatric one, demand clarity and consistency. The mental health professions have, however, failed to meet the first obligation of consciousness, which is to explicitly recognize and deal with the double bookkeeping embedded in the deep structure of Western consciousness.

In chapter 2, I consider explicitly some of the historical background that has led to this dilemma. The seventeenth-century philosophy of Descartes stated metaphysical dualism with almost coercive clarity. This dualism codified Western sensibilities so profoundly it was easily assimilated to the more general struggle between secular and religious thought. Subsequent centuries of philosophical work have not produced a single discourse that persuasively bridges the gap of dualism. Although phenomenologists, and others, have tried to undercut the intellectual habits that embody dualism, it is still true that one must, especially in mental science, be aware of tacking back and forth, and of the many temptations for self-deception embedded therein.

In chapter 3, I describe the most important theories of mental science in the last century or so, focusing on just how various theorists tried and failed to resolve the historically given intellectual dualism. Academic psychology, unlike the profession of psychiatry, has enjoyed the advantage of being free from a medical tradition that has combined medical treatment with entrepreneurial economics. The academic setting of psychology, in contrast to psychiatry, can and generally does avoid the pressures of professional profits and market economics. These pressures have become, at century's end, the control of medical payment by insurance companies and managed care corporations. This system is, however, only the last of such contexts for psychiatry, from which academic psychology has been shielded.

In this protected environment, psychology has produced many efforts to cope with mind–body dualism and with the anomalies thus produced. At its birth in the 1870s, psychology was "psychophysics," a discipline devoted to measuring mental perceptions of experimentally varied stimuli like sounds, lights, and weights. The mind's reckoning and the physical reckoning needed to be clarified with respect to each other. Gestalt psychology worked on dualism in a different way, and psychoanalytic psychology, cognitive psychology, and psychosomatic medicine each explored the dualistic gap—which is of course also a connection—between reality one grasps as mental and reality one grasps as physical.

Without a resolution, individuals must continually cope with dualism and its tacking. The "biological reductionism" of chapter 4 had been prepared for by nineteenth-century beliefs that mental disease is, finally, brain disease. But it also has roots in medicine and natural science, whose mechanical causality offers a vision of life as surely as it offers a vision of thermodynamics and other physical–causal–mechanical phenomena.

All reductionisms collapse various patterns of analysis to a single one. Biological reductionism is psychiatry's way of avoiding coping with dualism by simply reducing the two languages to one. Such reductionism is increasingly reappearing in academic and professional thinking as pharmaceutical treatments are refined. But the outcome of such reductionism is especially problematic; one's consciousness is not a thing, and the choices before an individual remain his or hers to make—despite causal mechanics.

In chapter 5, I trace the logic of dualism as it is handled in modern science, a logic of denial (that we dualistic are dualists) and a logic of reduction. Most notably, modern reductionism reduces human reality—personal meanings and experiences—to objects, and objects are, in a dualistic world, "not me" or "not us"—a construal which allows individuals to see others as "mere" objects, commanding none of the respect usually accorded to human beings. This objectification of persons opens the door to a particular violation of human integrity peculiar to psychiatry, of which lobotomy was the blatant version and psychopharmacology is the subtle version.

These violations are called, in chapter 6, *violence*—a term too raw, perhaps, to be thrown around, but useful in its accentuation of the costs of some aspects of current practice. Except for desperate social explosions, the violation of persons is always executed from a position of superior power. The mental health professions have this power, and they use it invisibly, such as in defining certain human problems as "diseases."

Like calling an idea a neuron, calling human perplexities and absurdities "diseases" jumps the mind–body difference mindlessly. Additionally, these struggles are engaged by a person trying to make sense (and failing), whereas diseases, in contrast, are contracted quite passively.[7] Such problems are more mental than physical, more personal and existential than biological. The violation or violence here is one of attacking parts of a person's mental life as if, like a disease, it deserves only to be obliterated, never to be taken seriously as a part of one's coming to terms with life.

The violence begins in theoretical sloppiness and eventuates in bad treatment. It comes from defining mental things in physical terms. This definition moves from moral issues of everyday life to scientific ones of causality with lightening speed and enormous persuasiveness. Eventually, it is clear that diagnosis itself, which medicalizes human tragedy and suffering, unobtrusively reduces moral and mental issues to technological ones. In the ideological attractiveness of science, condemning certain thoughts and feelings to the category of "disease" is concealed behind professional routines of healing and curing.

Of course, this practice obviously follows the format of "pathology" and "physiology," that is, of errant and dangerous deviations from complexly regulated organic systems of the body. When a cancer is cut out, the valuing of the regulated organic system over the dangerous deviation is hardly controversial. When, however, one masks or chemically ablates a personal struggle, the wisdom of such a

treatment might be questioned. To chemically alter human experience may, sometimes, be health-inspiring. At other times, it may
undercut essentially healthy efforts of a person to cope with existen-
tially difficult conditions.

Such treatments, when they clearly do this, violate the personal
and psychological integrity of the patient. The fact that such clarity
is rare testifies neither to the diseased nature of some symptoms nor
to a sound recommendation to eliminate them. Professionals have in
fact not looked very carefully. Any experience that is unwanted can
be seen as a symptom, and it frequently is so labeled. In practice, it
follows much too quickly that it is eliminated, and this is because
pharmacological agents have such power. Americans can master their
minds chemically the way they have mastered the physical world and
all of nature—physically. In psychiatry, this means chemicals for the
mind.

Also apparent is a dominant theme of mastering nature, which
enlivens all technological energies. The theme and the practice both
need to be questioned at this point. In chapter 8, I argue that the
absence of this questioning leads one astray, and the issue of violence
becomes even more urgent.

NOTES

1. Criticisms of psychopharmacology have been made before. Breggin
(1991), for example, is quite critical, and work by Ross and Pam (1995) certainly raise serious questions, as well as that of Brown and Funk (1986),
Fisher and Greenburg (1989), Fischman (1987), and Keen (1998). There
does not seem to be a rush of defense against these criticisms, perhaps
because the forces holding this practice in place are certainly, for the time
being, secure. I call attention to several efforts by psychiatry to deal with,
however, some of the difficulties: Azima (1961), Beitman and Klerman
(1991), Group for the Advancement of Psychiatry (1975), Karasu (1982),
Kass, Charles, Walsh, and Barsa (1983), and NIMH/NIH (1985).

2. David Healy (1997) noted, throughout his historically sophisticated
essay, the importance of this question. See also Keen (1998, especially pp.
67–71).

3. This line of thought has been elaborately developed by Szasz (e.g.,
1961, 1987), whose main works have been, in the latter twentieth century, a
staple in acquiring a critical attitude toward medical psychiatry. We are all
indebted to Szasz.

4. Of course, "pain" is an experience, and is already mental. The distinction between "mental" and "physical" pain may indulge a merely metaphoric use of the term, *pain*, in such a contrast. Nevertheless, the distinction still has a commonsense validity: A headache is not the same kind of "pain" as loneliness. A good collection of articles on this issue as it appears in psychosomatic disorders is found in Finell (1997).

5. This rather abrupt claim goes undefended here; the reader is invited to see the extent it might be justified by reading further.

6. I am of course aware that various "language games" or specialized jargons create many conceptual frameworks and discursive realms. I single out mental and physical because they are each very elaborate, coercive, and essential in modern (meaning the last three or four centuries) life, unlike other specialized discourses. These two also are particularly invisible insofar as they both have been reduced to common sense, and people have become adept at living simultaneously within the reach of both discourses without noting that they tack back and forth, nearly every minute of every day.

7. For one of a number of critiques of current diagnostic practice, see Sarbin and Keen (1998).

Chemicals for the Mind

chapter 1

SCIENCE, MORALITY, AND THE OBLIGATIONS OF CONSCIOUSNESS

PERSONAL PROBLEMS AND IMPERSONAL PILLS

Suppose I find myself awake at 5 A.M. and unable to get back to sleep. I am tired, but I toss and turn, and finally I get up. I wander around the house, hoping not to awaken others, and eventually I feel better—better than the vague sense that there is something terribly wrong. I cannot put my finger on what is wrong, and eventually the feeling goes away.

Suppose further that later in the day I am irritable to my wife, impatient with mechanical contrivances that do not work, and resentful of the time my job takes up. I have trouble concentrating on the job. I get frequent headaches. I feel tired all the time. I drink more alcohol. Sometimes I feel like crying, but I do not have any idea why.

If I take this story to my doctor, she may prescribe Prozac, or she may refer me to a psychiatrist who prescribes Prozac. After a few weeks of taking these pills, my sleep improves, I find myself interested in my work again, I cut down on my drinking, my wife and I laugh together, and the headaches go away. I have experienced what is called *depression*, and I have experienced the treatment most frequently given, psychopharmacological treatment, and I have experienced relief from my symptoms.

The only thing in my life that has changed from before my depression got out of control is that I now take pills regularly. My job is the same, my family is the same, and everything else is the same. I am satisfied with the treatment. But what about the rest of my life? What about the fact that my job contributes to the inexpensive production of running shoes that I recently read about, in the sweatshops in Singapore—that this system extracts an enormous cost from that population in order for the running shoes to be competitively priced. I try not to think too much about my job in these ways, but I visualize my own family in Singapore, my own children in the sweatshops, my wife and I ill from malnutrition, our parents long dead from food poisoning.

Of course, very few people have these thoughts, and I take comfort in the fact that they are not really relevant to *my* life. My job is to take the world around me as I find it, and to live as well, and for my family to live as well, as I and we can. I manage not to think too much about the sweatshops, about the accident of my own good fortune, and about starvation and suffering. I watch lots of videotapes and televisions shows, all of which distract me from these unpleasant thoughts. I am able to get them out of my mind.

That is, I am able to get them out of my conscious attention. Could these thoughts have something to do with my sense that something is terribly wrong? A year ago, I actually tried to bring this matter up with my wife and her brother, and the conversation did not get very far. In fact, I was ridiculed, and when I insisted we think about it, I was derided, called a "moralistic obsessive," and eventually ignored. This was upsetting in the short run, but I eventually mended the fences in these important relationships, and I know better than to bring it up again. My relationship with my wife now has this and other taboos; we have lost our earlier ease with one another. She knows I am critical and impatient and she walks on eggs, even though the worst of my symptoms are totally gone.

I even brought these thoughts up briefly with my doctor, and later with the psychiatrist. Each listened politely for a short while, then changed the subject. I came to assume, as they did, that worrying about people in Singapore was a part of my depression, and I became even more certain that I should not disrupt what remains of my ease with my wife, her brother, and myself.

PHILOSOPHICAL INFRASTRUCTURE

Psychiatric problems are moral as well as medical. There are cultures in which there is no distinction between the moral and the medical, but in Western cultures the distinction is inescapable. In psychiatry and psychology, the interior of both theory and practice must constantly tack between these frameworks, inevitably compromising one in the service of the other.

The example just given, shows a fairly common pattern of interpreting what might be called a "moral issue" as a medical one. Even as we say that we translated from "moral" to "medical" too quickly, it is clear that saying just that may translate from "medical" to "moral" too quickly. Maybe it is the case that my moral thoughts were symptoms of medical matters. Maybe I was depressed first, and as a result I worried about Singapore. It is not known which is the right frame for understanding my malaise.

Also common, however, is competent psychiatric practice, in which the content of my thoughts are taken seriously and explored. But at the same time, the psychiatrist, if she does her job, has to work her way to defining a medical problem in order for her expertise to be of relevance.

It would be a small matter to describe this tacking back and forth by revealing dilemmas in psychiatric practice. However, the depth of the disjunctions in one's understanding is both ingrained and pervasive. This manifest problem covers a latent one of historically accrued divergence between two kinds of human reckoning, in terms of two orders, or patterns of order, within which human experience becomes comprehensible. Sometimes reduced to the mind–body dualism of Descartes, the distinction is in fact as old as recorded Western thought.[1]

Philosophical language is often difficult, but it is clear how the pattern of meanings differs in the cases of thinking medically and thinking morally. In fact, these two patterns are two ways of understanding things, of making sense of life. These are, in fact, two orders of sense that have been inherited from the history of Western culture and philosophy (Fell, personal communication, 1997).[2]

Ordo cognoscendi is the order of ideas. It governs human thinking and knowing, which includes logic, mathematics, speech, and meanings. The order of idea is how individuals make sense of means–ends relationships, for example. If one wants X, one must do Y. Both "wanting" and "must do" are commonsense experiences everyone has every day. The order of ideas, in short, is how people think about behavior.

Ordo essendi is the order not of human ideas, but of natural things and events, an order that governs such natural events. Individuals construct nature differently from how they construct their mental lives. One billiard ball hits another, transmitting the energy of its motion, whether one wants it to or not, and whether one sees it happening or not. The "causality" here is independent of people, as are the rotation of the planets and the transmission of disease. This order is natural, a part of nature; it exists, and it simply is what it is, independently of anyone knowing about it.[3]

Human formulations of the *ordo essendi*—for example, theories of causality—must conform not only to events as they are known, but also to the order of ideas because the design of human ideas makes events intelligible. Human intelligibility depends on the order of ideas. Individuals understand medical science in the West rationally. Rationality is one structure in the order of ideas. Morality is another, and medical practice must also be moral, which is quite a different constraint. But like rationality, morality suggests an order different from that of nature and its mechanical patterns. And yet the order of ideas (i.e., rationality and morality) is entirely different from the order of natural events (i.e., causality). The order of ideas, including both rationality and morality, is a mental and a human cultural order. It is not a physical and extra-human, natural order.

The mutual dependency of the two orders on one another is impressive. The physical causalities (*ordo essendi*) that guide the earth's and the brain's evolution were necessary factors in the creation of human logic (*ordo cognoscendi*), and the rational logic of thought is a necessary condition for any reckoning of the causality in nature. But equally impressive is their difference in content. For all their interaction and interdependence, *ordo cognoscende* and *ordo essendi* offer vividly contrasting patterns of human comprehension. Human behavior is understood, for example, a temper outburst, medically (causally), and such a behavior is also morally (voluntaristically) understood. We understand it both as caused and chosen.

But these two understandings have very different implications. If the temper outburst is viewed as chosen, it would likely be seen as irrational and even perhaps as immoral. It would be judged and attempts would be made to correct it by persuasion to become rational, and moral. But if it is seen as caused, like a disease is transmitted, then it would be treated like anything else in the natural order. To change nature, one does not persuade or inspire or teach; one simply introduces a new causal agent.

In its *chosen* guise, human behavior either conforms to or violates rationality and morality, both of which offer a version of *ordo cognoscendi*. That is, behavior is understood to be either rational or irrational, and moral or immoral. In contrast, behavior in its *caused* guise is inevitable; there are no errors such as irrationality or immorality. Behavior is simply what it is; it does not point to a range of possibility (free will) from which it was chosen. Caused behavior is never immoral or irrational because both of these qualities are judgments that assume the leeway of *ordo cognoscendi* and not the necessity of *ordo essendi*.

The obligations of consciousness include being clear about this duplicity and the necessity to somehow manage it. It is not easy, however, and the reason for that, finally, is philosophical.

ONTOLOGICAL COMMITMENTS

To decide that the reality of human behavior is one way or the other is to make a commitment to one *ordo* or the other, and thus it is to make a commitment to a certain ontology, a theory of the nature of the being of human behavior. When one reckons the nature of the being of one's own decisions, one assumes he or she can choose among alternatives, and thus one commits him or herself to "the order of ideas," *ordo cognoscendi*. When one interprets the behavior of a client as inevitable, given his or her history and circumstance, one commits him or herself to "the order of events," *ordo essendi*. These inconsistencies may not be anyone's fault; humans have inherited these two ontological commitments, side by side, and shifting ground from one to the other is both common and problematic.

One could, of course, reflect on that seeing and interpret that shifting itself as either dishonest or inevitable, depending on whether one is committed to *ordo cognoscendi* or *order essendi*. One can also partial out chosen and determined aspects of any behavior. What cannot be done is to avoid making these commitments, even if they are distributed in complex ways. Individuals are not able, therefore, to escape dualism. The problems intellectually are insurmountable, and they are beyond solving finally. There is no reason anyone should be able to solve a 400-year-old (or 2,400-year-old) problem in a generation.

We should, however, face it.[4] Instead of facing the ontological question, as a culture and a collection of professions, humans mostly just indulge technology, which is to commit ourselves to that technologically driven commitment to the mere mastery of nature. The human mind (i.e., humans, in our motives) has objectified nature, and as our success in mastery has progressed, so has the realm of its applicability. Psychotropic drugs are a new frontier in the last half of this century, one in which humans are invading not simply the brain, but also the shape and tenor of human experience. The spirit of this invasion is the spirit of technological mastery, and it may be seen as terrifying as the atomic bomb. Furthermore, I cannot quite block the image of the poor dinosaur, whose awkward armor protected it so well that it finally became unable to cope with the tasks of survival. Sometimes, human mastery of nature appears exactly like that to me.

There is nothing astounding in this thought. It is conservative, iconoclastic, and like the early nineteenth-century Luddites and anti-industrialists, it is alarmist and perhaps squeamish. None of these features of my experience are either remarkable, nor do they make for an ontological commitment of which I can be proud. But I do think the invasion of humans' brains is an invasion of their minds, that a nation on Prozac is merely an extension of technology; it makes humans dependent, both like and unlike how they are dependent on electricity. It changes us. Sorting all this out is not really possible, and yet I cannot ignore the issue because there is too much at stake.

Like mastering electricity, manipulation of neurotransmitters promises to change the character of existence for our grandchildren. Indeed, it is already known as a version of exactly that same revolution that now brings television and other curses or blessings. Humans often have not been morally ready for their own power as a species, and they can become genuinely dangerous to themselves in their technological possibilities. To continue with psychopharmacological exploits is to tread near the arrogance of brain operations like the lobotomies[5] that disabled more than 40,000 Americans in the decade before 1955, when Thorazine, the first effective major tranquilizer, was introduced.

We are not only threatening to reproduce the lobotomy fiasco but maybe also the dinosaur fiasco—to not worry about this is to bury one's head in the sand. Extending technological power to chemical manipulation of human minds, with so little wisdom about the brain, not to mention so little wisdom about the intricacies of the mental landscape whereupon lie the moral coordinates of all one does—to expand technology this way is like riding down bigger and bigger hills on a bicycle in adolescent glee without noticing that one is out of control.

My philosophical commitment is to thinking about what we are doing to ourselves and to each other. I cannot say that the mental landscape is so sacred that it should not be technologically manipulated, for I have, as many have, seen how a little Thorazine can make the big difference between a person's ability or inability to function. I know that Prozac helps many people, too, and I am not willing to say it is simply evil to offer such help. I do not say that I have a commitment to preserving the unimproved condition of human mental life, even though there is little grasp of either the electricity or the morality of it.

At the same time, however, I cannot say that the lobotomy story and the dinosaur story are without warning.[6] Everyone walks an edge that is unstable, unclear, uncertain. Personally, I equivocate at the crucial moment. I think we all should equivocate, for that pause for reflection can, if we are to be saved at all, perhaps save us.

My philosophical position is that there is (being is) a question, a question already answered in the world's religions and cultures, but a question that nonetheless remains continually open to each generation, and to each individual in each generation. Who am I to become? That is the personal version of the question. More collectively, who are we to become? More abstractly, what is good? What is evil? More practically, how shall we organize ourselves? More clinically, how shall I cope with my distress? More professionally, how can I help you? These are all versions of what I call *the philosophical* and the *ontological question*, the question into which individuals are born, the question they face every day by virtue of the openings of the future, the question that makes them crazy, or, short of that, plagued with self-doubts, fears, and rages, the usual coping with which its manifestations have often enough been called *symptoms*.

Calling these struggles symptoms trivializes the question. It makes it into a small anomaly within an intelligible order. That intelligibility itself is in question, and yet it gets questioned only by philosophers and mad persons. It should be at stake in the symptoms we treat and the struggles we engage every day.

PROFESSIONAL IMPLICATIONS

Drug therapy is currently the most common therapy in psychiatric practice. In the end, the question of whether to use drugs to solve

personal problems should be in the hands of those with the problems, and not in the hands of professionals. In making this decision,
one is answering a question more deeply than what appears on the
surface. The face of it bears issues of tragedy and terror, or experiences that are not only frustrating but also are pre-emptive and
seemingly urgent. The obvious questions are ones like the following:
"Do I want to bother my friends, lovers, and family with the tasks of
engaging tragedy and terror?" "Do I want to spare them and myself
these things and go about other tasks that are important in their own
right—the obligations and commitments to childrearing, work, and
enjoying life—without having to take on tragedy and terror?"

Using drugs to cope with tragedy and terror can, it should be
noted, facilitate dealing with them, but such an eventuality requires
either extraordinary personal discipline or professional treatment
that combines drugs with insight psychotherapy. Both of these
requirements are rare; the prescription of drugs (more than 75% of
psychotropic drugs are prescribed by general practitioners) is usually
in place of, not supplemental to, insight psychotherapy.

Beneath these issues that lay on the face of the question of whether
to take or prescribe drugs are possibilities and necessities that characterize life in general.[7] Dwelling on these with any concentration and
effort reveals moral and philosophical decisions, such as how people
should shape who they are as individuals in a landscape of moral
options. There are possibilities to sacrifice one goal to achieve others; there are necessities to not sacrifice some goals; there are possibilities and necessities to decide what is important to pursue—and
thus who one is coming to be, in making decisions as one does.

When people take life's travails to clinicians, current clinical practice avoids these deeper issues. Professional help does not inform us
that the terrain one travels is both moral and medical, mixed in
dizzying ways. Instead, practice proffers a medical landscape of
symptoms and illnesses and treatments. The transformation of moral
and philosophical questions into technical problems of psychopharmacology has become the task of modern psychiatrists. These technical problems deliver clinicians from ambiguous and complex
questions to relatively simple ones, and ones that can be approached
by trial and error, as most prescribers necessarily do.[8]

Psychiatry advertises itself as a professional service that will take
on moral and ontological complexity in terms of technical and scientific tasks, and in doing this, modern psychiatry exercises its power
without considering the real questions, and without caring. All this is

hidden from practitioners and from the people practitioners help, and the hiding itself is hidden behind the face of the technological fix. Psychiatric training, with its pharmacological enthusiasms, is producing generations of psychiatrists who have not been challenged to understand much more than these enthusiasms.[9] Is the arrogance with which the pretenses here are practiced endorsed by those attitudes that championed lobotomy?

The neglect of the moral complexities in deciding to use medication to relieve the bite of personal and social problems follows from the medical language within which professionals understand these problems. Medical language is scientific language, and science (*ordo essendi*) is necessarily and appropriately mute about moral decisions (*ordo cognoscendi*). Medicine docs have a code of ethics, of course, but that code is limited to questions of what to do in the context of the project of curing diseases. For physicians to tell people how they should live goes beyond their expertise.

Who, then, are to be the consultants to whom people can turn to sort out the pros and cons of electing to take medication? The physician whose training and language are cast in terms of diseases and cures helps nothing more than the elimination of symptoms. Psychologists (as distinguished from psychiatrists), although trained in science, are not limited to science, and yet the additional training that some want to get in order to prescribe medication, for example, imitates medical education.[10] Such training offers no moral questions for either professional or patient. Who is to tell the professional that she or he is to tell the patient that the stakes here have to do with who one is to become? Preclinical training for psychologists may be more oriented to historical, political, and philosophical issues than is true for premedical students, but that is no guarantee of wisdom. In short, the decision to take medication for one's problems is nowhere addressed in its multiple dimensions for anyone who gets a prescription.

FAMILY IMPLICATIONS

The philosophical puzzles of *ordo cognoscendi* and *ordo essendi* also become very concrete and practical issues for a family that is dealing with a family member who is, for example, incomprehensible. An example of this is parents who are dealing with a daughter they do not understand, who violates her own goals by being inconsistent and confused, a daughter who has been diagnosed *schizophrenic*.[11]

Both parents and the daughter must cope with the issue of expecta-tions. Are the parents justified in expecting a certain amount of con-sistency from their daughter? Is the daughter justified in expecting a certain leeway from her parents?[12]

Presumably, the parents are sane and the daughter is not, but this does not answer the parents' question. If parents expect more than the daughter is able to deliver, their judgment that she is violating reasonable expectations may make her feel even less understood, more alienated, more angry, certainly hopeless. If, on the other hand, the parents expect less than the daughter is able to deliver, their defi-nition of her as disabled and defective will not be lost on her, and she may agree with them, thus giving in to "being crazy," or she may rebel against such judgments, to affirm her righteous indignation, or perhaps her self-pity, certainly her sense of not being understood.

How should parents gauge their expectations? In so-called normal family life, this decision seems to come about in due course. A schizo-phrenic daughter, on the other hand, confronts the parents with the awful and insoluble problem of whether to see her violations of their expectations in moral or in medical terms—in terms of the order of human experiences of rationality and morality or the order of things and their causality. Is her behavior because she is unable to do better? Or is it because she is unwilling to do so? Or is schizophrenia a disease that somehow affects their daughter's ability to exercise her free will?

If schizophrenia is a disease of the will, the causal order of things has disrupted the mental order of morality and rationality. This is possible; brain damage does this. But is schizophrenia a physical dis-ease? Research efforts to demonstrate that it is a physical disease hold out a hope; it is not a hope of cure, or even understanding. It is a hope merely of relief from the terrible ambiguity about how to gauge expectations of incomprehensible patients—and sons and daughters.

But do families of schizophrenics have an inescapable obligation to struggle with their children and themselves, no matter how exhaust-ing it becomes? On the one hand, it is clear that no one else in soci-ety has the obligation to this particular relative in the same way that her parents do. If parents do not sustain this struggle, who will? And if no one does, then what will become of the schizophrenic? Often the cost is already clear when families give up. Such a path may con-demn their children to permanent or sporadic care in a state hospital. But on the other hand, there must be limits to what is demanded of parents by children. Parents are not obliged to mortgage their entire future and happiness in what, in so many cases, looks like a lost cause.

If this issue is viewed in terms of *ordo cognoscendi*, then neither the parents nor the children can escape the responsibility of making a choice. If viewed in terms of *ordo essendi*, then both give up the struggle and accept the inevitable, telling themselves that nothing is, after all, in their hands. It becomes like the weather. No one blames some imagined weather maker; it is merely accepted. The human origin of behavior, understood by both parents and children, can and tragically does sometimes lose its interest to us. This mental origin becomes hidden behind a real or imagined physical one. When one retreats behind a mask of indifference, that mask threatens, finally, to become more than a mask.

THE OBLIGATIONS OF CONSCIOUSNESS

It was noted at the outset that the obligations of consciousness include the obligation to be clear about the duplicity one must deal with in the form of the very different languages of *ordo cognoscendi* and *ordo essendi*. To do that, to be clear about the duplicity, and to make a commitment to struggle with life in the face of it, as a parent or a therapist or a patient—to be clear in this way is to occupy the *ordo cognoscendi*. It is to be moral and it is to be rational, a choice from a range of options, in the face of this duplicity. Because the option always exists to take this position, individuals are making a choice even if they declare it is all a matter of mere natural causes. This choice emerges from a pattern that is shaped over time, distributing themselves between these two frames of reference.

The pattern is often a clear, free choice among alternatives. But another way of coping is to give the choice over to the world, so that one may say, "If she does this, then I'll see it this way, and if she does the other, then I'll see it the other way." This way of coping is also common, for it leads to a resolution, even if temporarily, and it frees one from the agonizing choice point that is so hard to endure. Giving the decision over to such events, however, sets up contingencies that could always be constructed differently, and so one's attempt to let the decision be determined by external events fails because one is always free to change the criteria.

So like it or not, the obligation of consciousness that emerged as most inevitable is the obligation to choose how to be conscious. The moral issue in the most blatantly medical situation is not escapable.

Individuals are condemned to be conscious morally. But of course there are various languages in terms of which to be morally conscious. One set is rationality–morality, a set where there is envisioned a standard right way to do things (the moral good) and to see things (the rational mind). Both of these languages offer a range of options from which individuals are obliged to choose. The most moral path or the most rational conclusion is not always clear, but these are familiar deliberations, made and then remade as time and results and patterns of reckoning them create the shape of one's personal consciousness.

Being conscious of one's consciousness must also include further sets of languages in terms of which to make choices. The language of hedonism, for example, offers a criterion that one rarely escapes and in some measure takes seriously. The "Good" and the "Rational" can be replaced by simply asking what is most convenient, or least distressing. Somewhat more complexly, it is always possible to define the "moral" or the "rational" as what is most pleasurable.

These various possibilities all exist for therapists and parents of schizophrenic patients. In the pushes and pulls of real life, parents are much more disoriented by these perplexities than are therapists. Therapists are professional, and their profession itself has its theories, its codes of practice, its ideologies. At any given time, one may be predominant. Currently, psychiatry leads the field with its medical language of causality. Firmly embedded in philosophical naturalism, psychiatry must nevertheless deal with the language of morality. Such language and the issues made clear by it are very inconsistently taught to psychiatrists in training, whose grasp of such issues seems much less important to the profession than their technical ability to eliminate symptoms.

The profession of psychiatry does not give adequate attention to the morality embedded in its practice. This is not a professional failure in any simple sense, for this profession is embedded in traditions of science and naturalism that find the language of morality anachronistic. In embracing these traditions, medical specialties are also enacting one of Western culture's central themes, that of the continuing growth of technological ability to master nature. In the conquering of disease, modern medicine is impressive indeed. The intricacy of the currently growing mastery of AIDS would have been impossible only a few decades ago. No one doubts the importance of this success.

But psychiatry moves from the body, which shares much with the rest of nature, to the mind, which is not simply a part of nature. Whatever else is true, the mind is that medium by virtue of which individuals have even a concept of nature, or of rationality, or causality, or human being.

By treating the mind as a part of nature, psychiatry is missing the moral dimension of its own practice. This is a practice that seems to dedicate technical mastery to making people's lives open to moral questions. But such a view depends on reducing consciousness to a natural object, and such a view practices that reductive theory by manipulating consciousness with drugs. It is as if consciousness were a squeak the machinery makes. Such a theory neglects the fact that human consciousness is not an object but rather is an individual's way of reckoning anything at all within understanding.[13]

NOTES

1. The claim in this sentence is a major thesis of this entire book. Any sweeping generalization such as this one obviously requires considerable development and argument. Although the statement here is relatively simple, the issues raised by it are not. I certainly do not exhaust the subject in what follows, but some of these issues do reappear for a fuller discussion.

2. Although the literature on dualism is voluminous, recent efforts to define the problem in terms of the kinds of discourse that codes the understandings of "medical" and "moral" matters seem particularly germane. Fell (1996, personal communication, 1997), drawing on the philosophy of Miller (1983), offered the analysis used here. The distinction between *ordo cognoscendi* and *ordo essendi* is Fell's, but he clearly drew on Miller and many other philosophers.

3. Fell (1996), who used this distinction between the *ordos* so powerfully, is among philosophers who see Nietzsche as introducing something new since Descartes (Prado, 1992, would say since Plato). For nonphilosophers like myself, and like psychiatry in general, Descartes seems to present questions that are merely academic. But my argument is that we are all implicit Cartesians, and to stumble on the limitations of that presupposed orientation to life, as psychiatry clearly does in practicing psychopharmacology, is to stumble on real problems in understanding, problems dealt with only by philosophers. I have found Fell's work helpful. I also recommend likely available works that have helped me, such as Prado's (1992) comparison of Descartes and Foucault, which is certainly another lucid reminder of the

limits of what we think we understand, and Voss (1993), as well as Watson (1987), and Sorell (1987).

4. Damasio (1994) is the most interesting current theorist who does face the problem of dualism. He stated: "Descartes' error remains influential. For many, Descartes' views are regarded as self-evident and in no need of reexamination" (p. 250). Damasio himself believes that cognition must be understood in the context not only of neurology, but also in light of the adaptive patterns of neurophysiological and rational adaptation. Critical of those who separate mind and body, he said: "Interestingly and paradoxically, many cognitive scientists who believe they can investigate the mind without recourse to neuro-biology would not consider themselves dualists" (p. 250). Although I agree with Damasio about implicit dualism, what I do not quite share his confidence that it can be overcome by studying neurobiology.

5. The lobotomy episode in U.S. and European psychiatry lasted for about two decades, from the mid-1930s to the mid-1950s, and has been described in detail by Valenstein (1986) and Shutts (1989). My earlier work on the topic (Keen, 1998) attempts to spell out some of the details of the debate in the context of psychiatry's struggle to incorporate medication into everyday practice in the last half of this century. See also Damasio (1994).

6. Blocking dopamine receptors with neuroleptics reduces psychotic symptoms in a majority of patients, and this certainly leads to short-term improvement. But in the longer term, this practice produces an up-regulation of the dopamine receptor system, which means that each neuron that seeks dopamine stimulation does so more avidly (Guttmacher, 1994). Several studies demonstrate that discontinuing use of neuroleptics leads more often to relapse with less stress than relapse for patients who had taken no neuroleptics for at least a longer period of time, such as a year or more (Birley & Brown, 1970; Chouinard, Annable, & Ross-Chouinard, 1986; Chouinard & Jones, 1980).

7. Sartre's (1956) many analyses of bad faith make clear that living honestly is complicated enough without drugs. Further reflection indicates that it becomes very much more complicated with them. If I pretend to be who I think you want me to be, I am behaving toward you in bad faith. This is true not only because I am deceiving you, but because, in forgetting that I am pretending, I come to deceive myself. My dishonesty comes to feel like honesty insofar as I see your confirmation of my false enactment of myself. My freedom is abdicated in favor of the comfort of your definition of me.

When I behave toward you under the influence of a drug, I have even less grounding in what criterion I should use in calling my behavior honest. If I please you, and I want to do so, then the self I am enacting may take root in my experience of success and come to stand as my best self, or my real self, or my ideal self. The drug has, under these conditions, complicated my self-deception, and ultimately it has further undermined my honesty. Sartre is not confident that non-drug experiences are ever free of these difficulties, but it is clear that drugs make them much worse.

Furthermore, what this situation does to human freedom is even more disabling. In order to be honest, I must recognize, and not hide from you, that I can be differently than you expect, that my "self" is ambiguous, still in the making, open to the future. But it is likely that my suffering from this ambiguity has motivated me to take a drug, so that my abdication of freedom is consolidated by the drug's ability to alter the shape of the freedom that ambiguity lends to my life. Insofar as ambiguity is aversive, we see here the makings of a serious psychological dependency on the drug, the convoluted layers of which are likely never to be unwoven. And the likelihood that the drug is permanent becomes real. See also Elfenbein (1995, 1996).

8. I again call attention to efforts to document this pervasive practice in the books edited by Elfenbein (1995, 1996), and a particularly poignant critique of these experiences is in chapter 4 of Karp's *Speaking of Sadness* (1996).

9. Indeed there is an abundance of fascinating issues in every phase of drug therapy. Take, for example, the process of developing, then authorizing, new drugs for the market. One aspect of this process are trials—specifically, randomized controlled trials (RTC)—which Americans, at least, do in an elaborate way. Healy (1997) pointed out that the U.S. input was unique in its collective approach to the issues. A number of coordinated programs link basic science testing to clinical evaluation, also using the multicenter studies in Veterans Administration Hospitals. Cole and Klerman (1964) conducted a nine-hospital study of chlorpromazine, finally settling the question of whether the new antipsychotics worked.

Despite these elaborate efforts, there are problems in the development of new drugs for the market. For example, Kuhn (1990) claimed that RCTs get in the way.

I had 40 patients in 1957 . . . without any control study, without placebo. It was only by clinical observation that I found something. The whole legion of researchers who work now . . . can only find an immense amount of facts, but facts which do not serve any practical result.

The problem was that the statistical data tended to outweigh the clinical data, so that the numbers seemed definitive on the question of whether, say, chlorpromazine works. Much to the embarrassment of psychiatry, this focus emboldened U.S. psychiatry to treat schizophrenics with Thorazine while remaining blind to the simultaneous creation of Tardive Dyskinesia.

An additional problem is that the RCTs lent themselves to the shortcut of comparing new drugs with ones that had been proved effective, and if no difference emerged, it was assumed that the new drug too should be authorized. But in 1980, this assumption was challenged by Paul Leber of the FDA. Healy (1997) said that Leber (1996) pointed out that the numbers involved in a traditional antidepressant trial made the lack of a difference between old and new treatments unconvincing evidence that the new treatment worked. Most such studies found differences in the side-effect profiles of the compounds. Thus, all the trials were doing was providing good marketing copy for the companies. Overriding much objection, Leber pushed through a formula that submissions must contain evidence of at least two pivotal studies—which meant studies that were placebo-controlled. The drug development plans of a number of companies were thrown into turmoil. Compounds that had come onto the market in Europe and become best sellers, for instance, never made it to the United States for this reason.

More problems emerge that can be ascribed to this specific context. RCTs have evolved as they did within a particular legal and medical-professional, and linguistic framework. What if the effects of these compounds were called *tension-reducing* rather than *disease curing*? Were this more likely to sell the product, it would have been so. Instead it has all been medicalized. Healy (1997) noted that "RCTs in conjunction with the restriction of prescribing to physicians, therefore, have powerfully reinforced categorical and medical models as opposed to dimensional models of psychiatric disease" (p. 103).

In this sense, Kuhn's comments at the meeting in Cambridge seem apposite and unsurprising. The result of the labors of vast numbers of researchers using ever more sophisticated scales has been the registration of compounds but not the advancement of science. Because companies do not care to prove that there are differences among their compounds, the marketplace is stuffed full of agents that are biologically quite heterogeneous, but whose clinical differences are minimized, indeed, left blatantly unexplored. All of this for the sake of grabbing a share of the big indication—which in psychiatry since 1980 has been depression.

10. The Prescribing Psychologists Register offers this training. I discuss it in my earlier (Keen, 1998) work.

11. Schizophrenia is more frequently diagnosed in developed than in less developed countries, and U.S. schizophrenics seem to have longer illnesses, and more severe ones. It is difficult to sort out whether U.S. culture produces more schizophrenia, or whether medical professionals simply diag-

nose it more often from a population no more ill than in less ineveloped countries. However, Castillo (1996) suggested that the "ego-centric" character of U.S. culture, compared to a more "socio-centric" culture in less developed countries, may account for the difference.

Expressed emotion (EE) has also been explored in the interior of families of schizophrenics. The robust finding is that high EE families (where emotionally charged comments are common, such as criticism, hostility, emotional intensity, or warning) produce significantly more relapses among recovering schizophrenics (Jenkins, 1991; Karno et al., 1987; Leff, 1989; Martins, de Lemos, & Bebbington, 1992).

12. Torrey (1988) has been particularly clear and helpful in discussing the problems and the options that face families of young people diagnosed as schizophrenic. One of the traditional, most torturous, dilemmas is nearing a resolution as Thorazine and similar medicines, which run a very high risk of a disabling side-effect called Tardive Dyskinesia, are being replaced by Clozapine, Olanzapine, and Resperdol, all of which are much safer. However, Degen and Nasper (1996) eloquently demonstrated that the new drugs fall far short of a final solution to the problems of any schizophrenic.

13. There are not many efforts to take up the intellectual task of righting our sorry theoretical confusion, but a very suggestive recent attempt is found in Schrag (1997).

chapter 2

ON DUALISM

Why Psychology Needs Philosophy

The advent and development of psychopharmacology in recent decades have brought into focus once again the theoretical problem of metaphysical dualism that so preoccupied psychology a century ago. William James, in his *Principles of Psychology* (1890), could not leave the topic alone, repeatedly struggling throughout his text to clarify, if not resolve, this ancient (Plato) and modern (Descartes) philosophical problem.

The current incarnation of the metaphysical dilemma reveals more than a theoretical conundrum. Psychopharmacology is a practice, not just a theory; it has become the first-line treatment in psychiatry; psychologists now want a piece of this action. And few among these practitioners, nor their researchers or theoreticians, appreciate the philosophical depth of the unanswered and usually unasked questions about what occurs during the practice of psychopharmacology. What is a mood? Is it caused? Or does it develop in a dialectic with the world? If the latter, then what does an antidepressant medicine do to that dialectic? Must science now become dialectical instead of causal?

Current theoretical options seem to be between organic theory, which claims that both the causes and treatment for mental illness must be physical, and psychological theories that focus primarily on mental development in explaining pathology and on interpersonal experience in treating it. Organic theory assumes that the brain is the "real" reality, and that "mental life" is merely a reifying name for its functioning. Psychological theory maintains that the physical reality of the brain is not the only reality. Psychological theories are not exactly dualistic, but psychology does in fact deal with what it believes are "real" and nonphysical factors, like conditioned emotions (Wolpe, 1982), repetitive relationships (Horowitz, 1988), and automatic thoughts (Beck, 1967).

These nonmaterial realities may be reduced to their physical manifestations, but they are known as experiences, or as acts, or parts of consciousness, or of a dialectic process, not as things. And yet they seem no longer part of a dualism, for psychology enjoys seeing itself as having left philosophy behind in its achievement of the status of science. This is true even of nonorganic theorists, who believe that psychological facts of one's conflicts with the world—instead of neurotransmitter imbalances—lead to abnormalities. This line of thought, implicitly or explicitly, criticizes organic reductionists for attending to the wrong "reality." Such criticisms of reductionism may be warranted, but they fail to see in the issue the historically accrued meanings that attend their critiques.[1]

DESCARTES' DUALISM

Descartes knew full well about mannequins, as did all learned men of the early seventeenth century.[2] Mannequins with moving parts demonstrated the use of pulleys and levers, but they served also as explanations of the human body. Science had progressed enough that the object world, including the human body, became, in the philosophical imagination, a mechanical contrivance, with certain properties that could be known by close examination. By the 1620s, this close examination of levers and pulleys was already under way, along with the mathematics and causal language of the time. However, when Descartes went beyond physics to philosophy, he had to deal with the mind that cognizes, as well as with the world's mechanisms that were to be known.

While adhering to the then obligatory theological connections of the mind to the human soul, Descartes clarified the metaphysical view, which laid down the major categories within which all reality was to be understood, primarily in terms of a dualistic, mind–body distinction. Things, *res*, were divided between material things, *res extensa*, and spiritual things, *res cogitans;* this distinction, one way or another, has continued to this day.[3]

The entire edifice of science is built on the notion that a person or a group of persons knows the object world. Implicit but so often unexamined by scientists is the knowing person, the knower. Much of modern philosophy is about knowing, but this work has not changed science's indifference to the subject. Until a better theory surfaces, this knower and this knowing are nonmaterial and quasi-spiritual, but they certainly must be counted, in some important sense, as "real."

Descartes' dualism constructed the knower as an entity, isolated and unified within itself, which knows the object world that it observes and thinks about rationally. This formulation may not be a good idea; it may involve "misplaced concreteness" in making knowing (the activity), content (the known), and the knowing mind that knows (the alleged agent of the activity) into spiritual entities, when they are not. Maybe the idea of entities is not a good one. But there nevertheless remain activity and conceptual content, if not an agent, that are real and, unlike *res extensa*, are a reality that are not extended in space.

The impressive achievements of science have made the explicit theory of mind–body dualism a relic of earlier times, not because science has a better metaphysical theory, but because science can proceed technologically to manipulate the objects in the world to human advantage without attending to such intricacies of the mind and its spiritual affinity to matters theological.

The most serious attention the mind has received by much science is the effort to make it more irrelevant, to make it transparent, to make it a nonconfounding nonvariable in the acquisition of knowledge, so that the knowing mind has a pure and uncluttered look at the object world it is examining. Thus has developed the elaborate methodological preoccupations of philosophers of science. Mind–body dualism is not a part of science, it is simply assumed by science, and it rarely comes up. The exceptions to this statement, of course, are those scientific attempts to reduce the mind to the brain, which is to erase dualism by fiat, leaving only the physics of light, the eyeball and optic nerve, brain chemistry, and behavioral outcome. But in this universe, there are no knowers.

There is also the application of the scientific method to "the mind"; that is, there is also "psychology," as it is now called. But this

science in this century has never taken seriously the strategic difference between knowing things in the world, on the one hand, and
knowing the minds that know, on the other. The more explicit psychologists become in erasing this difference, the more they make an
analogy between knowing things and knowing minds. I think it can
be said that this practice became absurd as we began "measuring" the
mind, along putative "dimensions," such as "intelligence" or "depression." If the commonsense notion that some people are more intelligent or more depressed than others leads to the scientific premise
that intelligence and depression are dimensions of the mind in the
same way height and weight are dimensions of the body, then common sense needs to be replaced in psychology by some very uncom-
mon struggle with the mind–body problem.

I do not, with these thoughts, intend to say that mind–body dualism is a correct metaphysical theory. But I do see it as practically an
inevitable one, short of denying consciousness altogether. I also
believe that this state of affairs grows from the history of Western
philosophy, and especially the intellectual development of science.
Progress in knowing and mastering the physical world has been such
a rewarding, often ecstatic, if not frenzied, activity, that the philosophical underpinning of science, which began as dualism and
remains a presupposed and unquestioned dualism, has gone unquestioned within science itself. Scientists are simply not taught to ask
who the knower is or whether science can do without such a figure.
They are taught instead to ask about things known and to ignore the
knower.

Of course philosophers have long known that there are intellectual
problems here, and many, such as phenomenologists most recently,
have sought to begin again to explore logically and historically issues
predating Descartes to find a less perplexing underlying theory than
dualism. Both Kant and Hegel offered systematic explorations of logical conceptuality (i.e., *ordo cognoscendi* instead of *ordo essendi*) as the necessary nonphysical foundation of science and knowing. The history of
philosophy is full of such serious and fascinating attempts, but they
have neither appealed to scientists nor been successful in competing
with science for air time in the intellectual marketplace of ideas.

NINETEENTH-CENTURY MORAL THERAPY

Thinkers in the early days of the theory of moral treatment, in the
early nineteenth century, thought in terms of the dualistic philoso-

phies of Locke and the priest Etienne de Condillac.[4] Insanity was thought to be caused largely by brain damage, for the insane brain fails to receive or react appropriately to environmental stimulation through the senses. "The intellect was a spiritual potential, which became act through the medium of the brain, just as volition became act through the medium of the limbs (p. 6)" noted Caplan (1969). Rush's (1812/1962) *Medical inquiries and Observations upon the Diseases of the Mind* speculated that the anatomical seat of insanity was the blood vessels of the brain. These theories are decidedly dualistic. "To believe otherwise is to advocate the doctrine of materialism, that the mind, like our bodily powers, is material and can change, decay, and die" (cited in Caplan, 1969, p. 7) said Amariah Brigham, first superintendent of the Utica State Hospital in New York in 1884.

Even though dualistic in their assumptions, most nineteenth-century theorists of the matter conceived of mental illness as organic. At the same time, either physical traumas or psychological ones like "sudden shock [or] . . . dwelling on powerful emotions such as fury, grief, disappointment, homesickness, terror, or religious fanaticism"[5] could cause derangement. There were other attending beliefs, less central but also speculative, such as the notion that the brain "consolidated itself" as experiences that accumulated in developing children, or the idea of certain faculties or traits becoming prominent— leading to the science of phrenology—and so on.

Phrenology supposed that exaggerated brain tissue yielded bumps in the skull that could be read as character and talent indicators. No one believes that today. In contrast, the notion of the brain consolidating itself in fact is mirrored in current understanding of childhood neurological development. For example, although all the neurons are present at birth, there are only 50 trillion synapses. In the first few months after birth, the number of synapses increases twentyfold, to 1,000 trillion. What was a preliminary organization of the brain is vastly consolidated early in life.

But what is most difficult to deal with in nineteenth-century theory is the idea that the mind, being of a different order of reality from the brain, does not become ill. The interpretation of "mental illness" in the nineteenth century as a disease of the brain seems to presume that the mind is hampered but not itself diseased. Its functional integrity may become disturbed, but that is only because the physical reality needs to be cured. If the piano is out of tune, the melody will be ugly. But the musician is sound—this dualistic analogy would say—awaiting a sound piano in order to offer a sound melody. Perhaps this bespeaks the preservation of the concept of a transcendent human soul.

In the nineteenth century, therapy, however, was not aimed at a physical cure of the brain. It was obvious that enough was not known to try to treat the brain directly. But improvement was nonetheless possible if the individual sufferer received quiet, consistent, morally felicitous experiences in the protected environment of moral treatment. Thus was born, to replace the dungeons of Bedlam, the "insane asylum," where sick brains could heal in the wholesome environment of a humane human community. And it sometimes was quite successful.

It is important to note that the *theory* of the cause of mental illness was the same then as is now seen in biologically reductive theories in psychopharmacology. Mental symptoms are present not because something called "the mind" is sick. The reason one is depressed is that he or she has a "chemical imbalance" in the brain. This theoretical consistency aside, the therapy in moral therapy was distinctly nonbiological. Since then, biological and neurological knowledge, ambitions, and confidence have soared.

Returning to the nineteenth-century view: If the mind does not become ill, but only the brain, whose material integrity is necessary for the mind to work properly, does this imply a "mind" that, as Brigham believed, does not change, decay, or die? Such an eternal "reality" is hard to substantiate or refute; any certain answer can be at best an opinion, but it can be said that Occam's razor would not abide it. Furthermore, this alleged immutability is hardly described in any persuasive detail. And yet, such a reality is never seen but is what actively sees. It is known to us not as an object but as the subject we actively are. For these reasons, such a reality as Brigham described would transcend the sort of science that depends on sense perception of the material world.

CONTEMPORARY IDEAS

By the end of the twentieth century, most of Western humanity views this sort of supposed "reality" as the mind, by virtue of which we know about more mundane, material "realities." This mind is available to manipulation in a fashion rather different from how individuals have come to master physical reality. One changes mental reality when one changes his or her mind, which is a direct action of the mind upon itself. One can decide, as William James said he did, to believe in free will. This is a route of access individuals "have" to mental reality. But it is more accurate perhaps to say that this mental reality is, in some sense, who one is.

It is also known that there can be considerable brain damage and disease without functional deficits showing themselves. This may be the current counterpart of the nineteenth-century view that in major mental illnesses, like manic depressive psychosis, the brain is diseased and it affects the mind, but even without physical intervention in the structure, the function can be restored through mental therapy. Even in psychosis, perhaps, there sometimes remain some ways one can decide who to be.

Despite popular ideas that the mind can change itself, contemporary scientists now are exploiting the fact that the mind can be manipulated in its mode of functioning by manipulating the physical (electrical, chemical, cellular, anatomical) brain. The metaphysical question of whether the "it" that functions through the brain is anything other than the brain itself returns one to the question for which there are reductive answers ("no") and more complex ones (versions of "yes").

When certainty is impossible, speculations are necessary. Ceasing to speculate, contemporary psychiatry is in the process of doing away with the mind by focusing exclusively on the brain. This "reduction" has consequences. For example, it has transformed medicine from a complicated study involving two perspectives, an external one of the outside observer, and an internal one of the person suffering an illness, to the terms of the external perspective alone. This strategy has eliminated the subjective aspects of the body such as desiring and perceiving, and it has focused exclusively on those aspects of the body that are lucid when one sees another from the outside.

There were notable conceptual gains (or at least changes) achieved in this move, which eliminated many beliefs and practices that took into account subjective aspects of the body. Understanding stopped tracking conscious moments in a stream of experiential order, and substituted "messages" sent by nerve impulses or hormonal "signals" that mediate events, say, in the hypothalamus and the adrenal gland—organs that are not experienced and yet are clearly important in the production of behavior.

This does not complete the elimination of mind from psychiatry. "Messages" and "signals," as concepts, might be understandable either as connecting subjectivities, a sender and a receiver, or as objective links in a causal chain, such as a "cascade of events" initiated by, say, a pituitary secretion. This ambiguity is being resolved in modern medicine in favor of the objective language, although the metaphors still suggest an understanding of the body as "trying to do something." Disciplined science completes the objectification by translating such notions as the body "trying to do something" into a language of energy—an impersonal mover, not an intentional subjectivity.

All this translation has enabled science to eliminate "superstitious" beliefs, having to do with the will of deities and the duties and desires of mere persons. It is a continuation of the scientific understanding of the body, which freed medical practice to develop into an objective science. Although the objective language made vivid part, but not the whole, of the body, it nevertheless facilitated the development of a medical technology that is historically new in the modern period and, of course, is very successful.

But the partiality at the basis of this language prevents its total success when it leads to such practices as surgically or chemically intervening in the brain in order to treat mental problems. A partially revealing language, no matter how successful in its own terms, may indeed run into its limits and not recognize them at all. Scientific enthusiasm can be blinding.

It is as if the science of acoustics, revealing both surprising understanding and impressive technical power in the manipulation of sound, were to say that its concepts and theory, of sound waves and temporal patterns, can reveal the central meanings of human speech. Such a science can indeed tell about human speech in its own terms, and that is hardly trivial. Sonograms allow the identification of individual speakers, in many species, and the ability to study changes in speech patterns that are caused by surgical experimentation, for example.

But scientists who do such work do not believe their acoustical science can reveal what is necessary to know in order to explore the meanings of words and the logic of theory and the motives of organisms who try to communicate with one another. To so extend the objectifying science into realms of meanings and motives is to claim too much for a partial perspective. It is to persevere in a metaphysical belief about reality, a belief that states, quite wrongly, that its perspective is not partial.

Psychiatry, in reducing the mind to the brain, in reducing human experience to physical events, in reducing struggles with human problems to chemical imbalances in the brain, is like a wildly ambitious acoustical scientist who proposes that his or her science can replace experiential understanding of language. Maybe it is wise to opt for nonreduction, even if it imitates a dualism, for such an option envisions a mental reality that is not a thing, which is nevertheless known, and that transcends that manipulation of the physical world about which modern humans have so much hubris.

Breggin (1994) has argued that pharmacological therapy in psychiatry damages the brain rather than cures it, and in fact there is as much circumstantial evidence for that interpretation as there is for the notion of cure. The continuing refinements in medications thus aim to damage the brain in such a way that the functions that are lost are necessary for symptoms, but not for ordinary experiences. Because unwanted psychotic symptoms are very close to dreams, imagination, and other healthy experiences, it is not likely that this will ever be done very well. Having seen medication "work," it is impossible to justify, in terms of current data, the term *cure*, or to refute the term *damage*.

Whether Breggin is right or not, however, leaves the problem of how to talk about mind and brain without reifying both. However, in order to argue that what is referred to as the "mind" is nothing but the brain's functioning (a "squeak the machinery makes," perhaps), it would be necessary to justify scientifically the notion that antipsychotic medication, when it works, cures rather than damages the brain. For, if it is allowed that damage cures, then the case becomes stronger that one should speak also of some other agent than the brain, which acts through the brain, but can manage many functions even with a partly damaged brain.

In any case, it is obvious that the mind depends on a degree of integrity of the brain in order to be sound. Because medical manipulations make the brain more commonly less intact, something with integrity maintains its way of doing what it does even in the face of damaged organs. The theorist most attuned to such a line of thought is Sacks (1970), who continually focused on *the person's* response to disease as well as on losses caused by the disease.

That something that maintains its integrity, or what it can of its integrity in the face of damage, may be nothing more than the functioning of the brain itself. And it cannot be said that operations and medications to cure epilepsy do not work, nor that every brain is naturally intact until it is messed with. But one is obliged to ask whether treatment of the feelings and beliefs of depression, for example, when they are altered by antidepressant medicines, change a thing, like the tuning of a musical instrument, which then alters a function.[6]

Or does some other, mental integrity try to maintain itself in certain ways even as it gives up other aspects of its former way of being? Or might it be said that that integrity is like the functioning of any other bodily organ (e.g., the kidney) that, in the face of a trauma, infection, or other damage, performs as closely as possible to how it usually performs?

If dualism is avoided by opting for that last conceptual strategy, one must ask whether one is in fact avoiding dualism. For the language in terms of which one understands the functioning of such restorative efforts and integrity of the brain (but not the kidney) is exactly the interior language of mental life. Mental life is crucial to understanding persons, and understanding of persons will never be adequate without such language. More philosophically, it must be added that the order of language is itself a logical, conceptual order rather than a material, causal order of the physical world (*ordo cognoscenti* rather than *ordo essendi*).

It is arresting to note that depressed persons sometimes commit suicide. Presumably, they would not do so if they were not depressed. But suicide is not somehow an effect of a prior cause in anything like the way physical cause and effect are understood. It is a decision, made by a mind that is conscious of itself, to be differently, or, depending on the case, to stop being. It cannot but be understood as a decision to kill one's own body, and thus to end oneself. The mind can do this, as surely as a brain disease can kill the mind. But if one says that a brain decides, in the intentional way the mind does, one has become wildly metaphoric. The brain is an object, whose action is known in the language of chemical and physical causality, not in the language of decision making. To kill one's body is a decision, not a mechanical effect of an infection or a tumor or a brain disease.

The analogy that the mind is to the brain as the melody is to the piano may make multiple points of sense, but it also complicates our theoretical dilemma. The act of suicide says that the analogy of music to mind and instrument to brain is too simple. A musician can decide to stop playing. Such a figure introduces a third term, or a stronger second term—one who is an *agent*.

UNDERCUTTING DUALISM

How did this position of such theoretical obscurity occur? There are answers to this question at many levels of detail and expertise. At the very least, it must be said that it has to do with our neglect of philosophy in the face of the technological achievements of science. As humans, we came to know the world very well, and we developed many hammers to shape it to our will—including ways to shape the operations of science itself. The more we perfected our manipulation of the material world, the more hammers we developed. Eventually, science came to look like our most impressive intellectual achievement, and we forgot about the consciousness that made it all possible. When the only tool one has is a hammer, all the world, including even one's own mind, begins to look like nails and horseshoes. The scientific errors involved in the tragedies of lobotomy are of this nature. We are not much further advanced philosophically than we were 50 years ago, and so it is far from clear that we are not committing the same errors with our latest technology of pharmacology as we did in the disastrous mutilation of brains that came from the surgical hubris of lobotomists.

If we want to develop a language that would bridge chemicals and experiences, instead of merely reducing experiences to chemicals, we shall have to do so philosophically. Data from science committed to a neglect of philosophy can accumulate forever without challenging its own philosophical assumptions.[7]

As an attempt to broach dualism philosophically, I mention the work of one philosopher (out of several possibilities) whose career was spent dealing with exactly such issues as he had inherited them from the history of philosophy. John William Miller (1983) argued that self-control (i.e., freedom) is the center of human being and of the disciplines that study human being, such as psychology. The assimilation of psychology to a scientific framework that denies this center limits psychology's ability to understand its object: the human psyche.

In an original and telling line of philosophical thought, Miller worked toward integrating the human psyche and the object world that it knows; Miller worked toward overcoming what appeared to be a difference so drastic (such as the fact that a thing is extended in space while a mind is not) as to force individuals into dualism. The more one denies one's dualism, the more firmly entrenched it becomes. The more firmly entrenched dualism is, the harder it is to overcome the intellectual inability to understand either objects known or the knowing subject. Dualism, compounded by the denial of dualism, certainly is ill-equipped to see the meaning of psychopharmacology.

Appreciating the dead end of dualism, and even perhaps its tendency toward violence, Miller argued that one must begin with the functioning unity of the person. Much of the history of Western philosophy has analyzed the person into parts, a mental and a physical, based on lines laid down in the earliest consciousness of philosophy. The very first philosophy, a kind of spiritualism, saw spirits and intentions everywhere. Like all historical adventures, human philosophical thought advanced through criticism of its forebears, leading to a second philosophy of naturalism, the center of which was a totally unintentional world of nature. In the face of naturalism, against the backdrop of spiritualism, it was inevitable (or seems at least in retrospect to be so) that philosophy would gravitate toward a combination of intentional spirituality and mechanical nature (Fell, 1996).

Of course the history of philosophy is enormously complex, but this historical pattern, studied by philosophers, predisposed subsequent formulations to be dualistic, or to be critiques of dualism, or to be rebellions against or reaffirmations of dualism, never completely leaving it behind. Modern science is, of course, adamantly naturalistic, but like so many naturalisms of the past, its philosophical basis has not resolved dualism but instead merely affirmed the mechanical and material character of nature. And it has neglected the consciousness whereby and wherein nature matters.

Meanwhile, natural scientists are, of course, conscious and so they enact the dualism for which they have no philosophical language. Like the alcoholic in denial, who secretly drinks and depends on alcohol even as he or she affirms his or her sobriety, science's uncompromised focus on exploring nature denies the presence of the factor that makes it possible. In denial of mind, science's own effort is inexplicable to itself, and the task of integrating mind into natural science takes seriously neither the uniqueness of mental life in nature nor its integral intertwining with nature. The philosophical task of integration remains neglected.

But the philosophical and scientific failure goes beyond denial of "mind" in this sense. It extends to a misreading of the body, as if the body were not a minded body, as if it were a machine. Most obviously, the body functions, and the patterns of its functioning conform to patterns of machines. Less obviously to mechanistically predisposed scientists (but quite obvious to philosophers like Merleau-Ponty,[8] Miller, and Fell), the body follows other patterns of functioning that look at the world, act on it, speak about it, and so on.

The human body is embodied mind and will, the locale and the vehicle of mind and will. It's the minded body that acts, that is, human agency, and that is, simply, the agent, the functioning person or individual.

Fell's comments continue:

Any sharp distinction between "the mind" and "the body" comes after that, and so is talk about two already-interrelated aspects of the agent, the person. Although all the evidence shows this, the massively influential assumption of an eternal and separable soul has served to compromise and obscure that evidence. (Fell, personal communication, 1997)

Undercutting dualism is not an advanced project. However, some philosophers are acutely aware of the task. To take seriously such an alternate starting point for psychology would lead first of all to the affirmation that "embodied will" indeed does describe one's experience. If I want (will) to look, my body orients and gazes, and "I" look. At that moment, I am a looking body. The former incommensurate languages of (1) experience as experienced: "Blue sky with clouds gathering ominously in the west" and (2) physical events: "retinal cells firing as stimulation by light focused by the lens, leading to optic nerve and occipital lobe activity . . ." are each clearly opting to look at that part of my "embodied willful looking" in which their languages each specialize.

Each of these languages can be replaced by a third language of embodied willful looking that lacks their detail. The first two, specialized refinements offer an abstract language suitable for some settings, but they falsify my willful, bodily looking. The first language explores the appearance of weather, the second neurophysiology, both important human experiences and traditions. Omitted from the language of both is the larger experiential structure of willful embodied looking. The weather-interested language takes the physiology for granted, and the physiological language takes content for granted. But both take for granted the human epistemic situation of willful looking as a body.

In these two specialized languages, the whole of the experience of bodily looking and willful seeing is not articulated. Instead, each of these languages articulates parts that can be abstracted out and laid out as descriptions that magnify some features and obscure others. Least magnified and most obscured is the "act" of looking. That act, and all acts, are at once willful and corporeal. An act engages mind and body in their predualistic unity.

If the continuing refinement of psychopharmacology eliminates side-effects and more precisely targets what are called *symptoms*, a theory of embodied human action that so far does not exist will be needed even more urgently.

NOTES

1. The problem of dualism is obviously not that it is a true or a false theory. Its statement by Descartes, and its incorporation into language are related, but they are not the same thing. Descartes can be refuted, and I accept Heidegger's (1927/1962) general approach to such a refutation, which states the human consciousness and the world stand in a relation that is not accurately described by the categories, moral and medical, nor by the Cartesian opposition of mind and body, or more generally, subject and object.

According to Heidegger, the philosophical abstraction, "object," implies a mode of existence that contradicts his theory of human being. *Dasein* apprehends objects, but an object is, originally and tellingly, first encountered *zuhanden* and not *vorhanden*, which in turn implies an attitude of involvement with, and action in terms of, such an object. This primary relation to the world characterizes the fundamental data of human experience and philosophy. Thus, Descartes already assumed what he apparently concluded, that (a) subject and object are opposites, (b) the subjective grasp of the object is spectatorial and not pragmatic, and (c) the two touch one another from a position of separateness. Heidegger, beginning phenomenologically, obviously avoided this traditional assumption.

The evolution of language, however, has not done so. Descartes' philosophy is incorporated as a complex of assumptions, not as an explicit philosophical theory. Collectively, then, speakers of Western languages accept implicitly, as an unexamined step, the dualistic creation of (often) explicitly rejected, but unconsciously embraced, separate world designs, that of causal natural science and that of moral common sense. These separate worlds are codified in discursive practice, and they yield everyday absurdities.

These absurdities, as they appear in ordinary Western experience, must simply be accepted as part of the mystery of life. This is because we have embraced science uncritically, adding its specialized discourse to our already existing way of speaking, thus perpetuating a dualism experientially and discursively, but not at a level of conscious critical thought that makes lucid the bad fit between the two.

Heidegger (1982) is accompanied to various degrees and in various ways by Jaspers (1975), Marcel (1964), Sartre (1949), Merleau-Ponty (1964), and others in the phenomenological and existential effort to deal with dualism. This philosophical effort, however, has not had the effect on Western common sense that natural science has had, although it does continue to matter as a critical moment in Western reflection on the self-world relationship. Merleau-Ponty's statement is perhaps the most persuasive, in his description of individuals' "operative intentionality," with which they commonly engage the world. This experience precedes, and must precede, the reflective detachment within which one allows oneself the luxury of detaching subject and object. Beyond this, Merleau-Ponty's "knowledge in the hands" is picked up in Wittgenstein's "I really do think with my pen, because my head often knows nothing about what my hand is writing" (cited in Cooper, 1990).

2. For sources on Descartes, see note 3 in chapter 1. With respect to American psychology, William James offered a prebehaviorist discussion of issues that, at the turn of the twenty-first century, remain important, although psychologists rarely tend to them anymore. Reading James' psychology (1890, 1892) reveals again and again that some crucial metaphysical question, such as whether or in what sense the mind is autonomous from the material lawfulness of the brain, receives an equivocal answer. On the one hand, the activity of the mind is "uniformly and absolutely a function of brain action, varying as the latter varies, and being to the brain action as effect to cause" (James, 1892, p. 6). This "working hypothesis of this book," however, is not taken by James to be the final formulation of the truth, and in fact he later pointed out that

the whole feeling of reality, the whole sting and excitement of our voluntary life, depends on our sense that in it things are *really being decided* from one moment to another, and that it is not the dull rattling off of a chain that was forged innumerable ages ago. This appearance, which makes life and history tingle with such tragic zest, *may* not be an illusion. (James, 1892, pp. 237–238)

3. I am, of course, simplifying Descartes without, I hope, being inaccurate. The complexities of Descartes lie not in what he concluded but in the laborious pains he took to establish these two realities. My main source here is *The Meditations: Concerning First Philosophy*. A very useful edition is translated and edited by Laurence J. Lafleur (1964) and published under the title: *Descartes: Philosophical Essays*. It is noteworthy that "mind" is clearly in place

by the third meditation, but the establishment of "matter" must await the sixth. In the meantime, he must, as a seventeenth-century philosopher, deal with the existence of God, His perfection, and so on.

4. Ruth Caplan's (1969) *Psychiatry and Community in Nineteenth-Century America* is a particularly helpful book on these matters. However, my favorite historian on these matters is Andrew Scull (1989), whose *Social Order/Mental Disorder* and other writings (1972, 1985, 1987) reveal the real intellectual leverage afforded by historical research.

5. Caplan, *Psychiatry*, p. 7.

6. There are suggestive data to this effect. See Baxter et al. (1992).

7. Current psychological studies of "stress" seem to bridge the mind–body gap in making the concept refer simultaneously to neuro-hormonal and mental events. Medical consequences of stress can never be lucid without taking stress seriously as mental—as meaningful experiential phenomena.

Relations between the immune system and both psychological and neurological systems are complex and only in recent years coming clearly into focus. Because of the interactions of these formerly assumed-to-be independent systems, stress makes one more vulnerable to illness (Ader, Felter, & Cohen, 1991) and illness probably makes one more vulnerable to stress. Mental aspects of stress have fairly well-known neurological and hormonal correlates, which in turn affect the immune system, so there are here, as elsewhere, good reasons to try to work on apparent causation across the boundary of language separating mental and physiological events. Psychoneuroimmunology is a modern version of psychosomatic medicine first envisioned by Alexander (1943).

It is interesting that the term *stress* is almost unique in having simultaneous meanings in both mental and physiological discourses. Many emotion words are approximately like this, but unlike the general notion of stress, emotion words tend to name specific cognitive content as well as the general experience of stress. Anger, for example, is imprecisely distinguishable from fear in terms of physiology, but the two are distinctly different when they are taken in their full experiential splendor.

Cognitive labeling of one's own experiences, however, is sometimes quite difficult as well. Am I primarily angry or afraid when facing unjustified attack from another? Rarely is there a clear single answer.

8. See Merleau-Ponty (1963).

chapter 3

PSYCHOLOGY'S STRUGGLE WITH DUALISM

We may understand the two incommensurate realms of physical reality and mental reality as specialized ways of experiencing human reality in the modern period. These are made possible by separate discourses and traditions. One of these is natural science, and the other is an older traditional mode of expressing one's mental content.

This chapter shows that this problem, which has no clear and popular name, has nevertheless been a crucial, underlying, sometimes explicit but often implicit, issue in the very invention of psychology as a science, a practice, and an academic discipline. Mental life and the mechanics of the physical world are described in different discourses, which construct different worlds. But they come together in psychology, which studies the former with methods from the science of the latter.

The former is the older kind of discourse, and yet as one looks at the discourse of premodern times, one sees a way of experiencing human reality that does not separate dualism as sharply as is done in the modern approach. For example, Aristotelian science, from the modern point of view, is a confused mixing of what we call mental concepts like *telos* (purpose, intention) with physical concepts like number and weight. When things are said to have purposes, as Aristotle sometimes said of them, it is anachronistic to modern sense; to see purposes in things is to misperceive, for purposes are not in the thing itself but in the seeing.

Furthermore, we are both proud and embarrassed by the achievement in the seventeenth century of purifying the two categories into the modern distinction between things extended in space and things mental, in the mind, which occupy no space. Our pride is in the technical abilities of our science; our embarrassment is in our dualism, which we rarely admit and even more rarely try to deal with.

The mastery of the physical world has always been useful. Western sciences have elaborated ancient concepts of number and physics into the invention of, and the mathematics of, machines. This has been one of the main achievements since Descartes' dualism facilitated the concept of nature as itself a machine. Mechanical relations of cause and effect characterize the discourse of science, whose frame of possibilities facilitated the elaboration of physical laws. These laws grounded modern knowledge of the physical world, expressed in mathematical relations, and they portrayed a mechanical order that governs physical reality, everything from the wheels in a watch to the rotation of the planets.

This scientific language, in its modern version, omits not only Aristotle's *telos* (his term for the purposefulness of natural events) but also human purposes, as well as desires, feelings, thoughts, ideas, and certainly those moral and aesthetic realms of the good and the beautiful that open into the earlier encompassing order of religion. Most importantly of all, knowing, as the activity within which all this language operates, is either not explored, because it takes place in that nonspatial, mental realm and hence is not amenable to science, or knowing is construed as an activity as mechanical, predictable, and calculable as the physical world that is known.[1]

Modern scientific language has specialized in the physical world and not the mental life. It demarcates a specialized way of experiencing and endorses its verifiable content as "knowledge"—as opposed to beliefs, faith, opinion, value judgments, emotions, desire, and so on, all of which are devalued and at best made irrelevant to the serious knowing that masters the world. At worst, nonscientific experience is seen as antagonistic to serious knowing and hence must be curbed on every side, to protect oneself against that error that would interfere in the mastery of the world.

MENTAL SCIENCE

In psychology, as it is taught to contemporary students, the language of the science of the brain is the language of mechanical cause and effect—refined into elaborate concepts about chemicals, neurons, and electrical impulses, and about neural transmission in the brain. Furthermore, first-line treatment of more serious mental disorders, such as schizophrenia, intervenes in this machinery in various attempts to change neural and chemical events in the brain in a curative way. In light of how little is actually known about the details of brain functioning, there are surprising successes in such treatments, although by no means do these approach the traditional notion of a cure.

Schizophrenia is the most common diagnosis of severe mental illness. It is not known whether this term refers to one disease or many. Only a minority of psychiatrists and psychologists examine the mental functioning of schizophrenics with enough detail to conclude even elementary things, such as whether the patient is "better" or "worse." For the most part, professionals, like the rest of us, depend simply on common sense to judge the amount of independence that patients can be granted. Those who struggle with such issues must work in a fashion of double bookkeeping, juggling the incommensurate languages of cause and effect in neurotransmission, on the one hand, with the language of desire and terror and belief, on the other. Presently, to describe a mental experience like a delusion in terms of physical events like neurotransmission in the brain, at what site, involving what chemicals, under what specific and general neural conditions, is about as far from our ability as measuring the will of God.

But in psychology and psychiatry, scientists must face the fact that treatment goals are mental, whereas their language of science specializes in physical reality. Pharmacological means for reaching a mental goal is also physical. Scientists can, if they persist, proceed by mere trial and error, so that they will eventually be able to say, with a certain probability, that so many milligrams a day of Drug X will eliminate a delusion, given certain other gross conditions such as the history of delusions in this patient, and so on. Such trial-and-error science can yield practical results, and it can even yield theory, but such theory is always obligated to do what cannot be done theoretically—translate from the language of physical science to the language of human experience. Hence, there is no such real theory; there is no modulus of translation.

EARLY MENTAL SCIENCE

Efforts to bridge this gulf were first tried in Western psychology at its birth in Germany in the nineteenth century, in the science of "psychophysics." In that effort, "laws" were formulated that describe the quantitative relation of physical changes in a stimulus to mental changes in the experience of that stimulus. The term *psychophysics* expresses the hope that mind–body dualism could be resolve through the collection of data. By the end of the nineteenth century, researchers knew how to quantify mental judgments of pitch and loudness, for example, and they could also quantify these same variables as physical dimensions of sound. It seemed only common sense that these two quantifiable variables, the mental and the physical, could be systematically related to one another under a variety of conditions, and a start could be made in developing that bridge of knowledge that could connect heretofore conceptually separate realms of physical and mental events.[2]

Weber's law stated that there is not a simple one-to-one relation between a change in a physical stimulus (e.g., heaviness of a weight) and a person's perception of it. If I am holding a weight of 32 ounces, and the scientist adds to it out of my line of vision, I am unlikely to detect an increase (a just noticeable difference [jnd]) until that increase is 8 or 9 ounces, or about one quarter of the 32 ounces. If, however, I am holding 8 ounces, the jnd will be close to 2 ounces. The threshold for a jnd, then, is not a function of the absolute size of the change, but rather it is a constant fraction (about one quarter) of the standard with which one starts.[3]

Weber hypothesized that this sort of finding existed in the loudness of sounds, the brightness of lights, and all areas of sensual consciousness. Many of these findings were in fact produced. It was, however, not Ernst Heinrich Weber but rather Gustav Theodor Fechner who parlayed this finding into a vision of a new science that could close the gap between mental and physical events. In fact, Fechner was passionately dedicated to both science and to the philosophy of Schelling, and he suffered much from the disjuncture of his two passions. His 1860 book, The *Elements of Psychophysics*, included extensions of this logic into esthetics and eventually into spiritual truths more like Schelling than Weber. Many scientists accepted his method and his hope, but not his conclusions. Thirty years later, James pronounced the entire effort worthless.[4]

For his part, James could never defeat dualism from within science, so he simply lived with it. His *Principles of Psychology* (James, 1890) never tires of returning to the theoretical problem, such as how to understand an emotion, an event known from both the side of the physical science of physiology and from the side of conscious experience. But his resolution, if ever it emerged, is in his philosophy of action, which he called *pragmatism*. Although pragmatism became an important philosophy, it also never did for the divided culture that which Fechner had so dearly hoped could be produced in the psychological laboratory.

The point of this nineteenth-century European and American effort eventually got lost amid other developments in psychology. It came to be no longer believed that psychophysics could elaborate laws as readily as had physics, for the discipline had floundered. The solution required, then as now, conceptual breakthroughs. In the absence of ideas about how perceptual content is related to brain events, research lacked the level of theory that could guide psychophysical research beyond fairly trivial findings.

Psychology, therefore, was, early in this century, facing a road block. Various innovations were often more interesting than the psychology that became dominant in the 1920s and continued as the dominant paradigm until the 1950s: merely reductive conceptualizations that solved the problem by eliminating "mind" as a remnant of an earlier prescientific age.[5] Behaviorism became the center of American psychology.[6] E. C. Tolman was the most successful of a small band of behaviorists who kept "mind" in mind.[7]

Behaviorism, of course, is cast in the strictest scientific language. It often seemed, despite references to mental life now and then, to be a science closer to physics than to any other. In fact, Watson's (1924) enormously controversial *Behaviorism* is reprinted by the University of Chicago with the subtitle "The book that initiated a revolution in its attempt to make psychology an objective science." Insofar is this revolution succeeded,[8] only experimental studies that were behavioristically pure were allowed to be printed.[9] For some journals, this was the case for several decades, and textbooks to this day announce a primary commitment to science without noting any difficulty dealing adequately with "mental life." Psychology has flourished in the academic world, in medicine, and in the popular culture with an elephant in its living room. Like the proverbial such elephant, no one seems to notice this obstruction, even though they must always walk around it and even though they are blocked from some paths of inquiry.

It is easy to be cynical about behaviorism and its rather uncompromising rejection of mental life as relevant to psychology. But during those decades, from 1925 to 1950 or 1955, the behaviorist program inspired an enormous amount of research about behavior, especially that of animals.[10] The historical legacy must be said, however, to include not only a neglect of mental life but also a profound theoretical bias that implied or stated that the only psychological reality was that reality intelligible within the language of the physical sciences.

GESTALT PSYCHOLOGY

Through the 1930s, especially in Europe, the behavioristic enthusiasms were shadowed by Gestalt psychology,[11] another serious attempt to bridge the mind–body gulf. There were two basic data. First, a puddle on a level, flat surface becomes perfectly round. There are, in the physical universe, laws of gravity and other forces, resistances, and so on, that are organized at the higher level of a pattern of roundness. The roundness, or symmetry, is at once the product of separate forces and at the same time it is an actualization of the superordinate physical law that nature balances itself, organizes itself into fields of equally distributed force and resistance that display order and wholeness.

Second, the human perceptual field organizes the objects in its scope in the same way. Figures that are roundish are seen as round; a gap is closed to make it whole in experience even though the gap is clearly visible. A collection of spilled beans makes a pattern that is seen, and once it is disturbed, other patterns are seen, rather than the random distribution of beans that is actually there. Thus again, as in psychophysics, a surprising and unexpected similarity appears between physical events and the perception of them, between the physics and the psychology that are, for mysterious[12] reasons, separate sciences.

For Max Wertheimer, Kurt Koffka, and Wolfgang Koehler, the insight into a pattern that bridged mental and physical realms was too tempting to let go. The order of the balance of forces in the solar system is congruent with not only one's perceptual world, but also with the mathematical rationality of the study of physics. It was, of course, again the Germans for whom this was a fascinating breakthrough. Wertheimer, Koffka, and Koehler, among other Jewish immigrants to the United States in the 1930s, populated U.S. universities and U.S. psychology with another hope of overcoming the mind–body gulf. The enthusiasm of these scientists caught on in America much more than did the complexity of theory with which Gestalt psychology struggled with its task. In fact, most Americans were not interested in resolving a philosophical issue that seemed to be irrelevant to behavioristic experimentation or to the Freudian analysis of dreams and other bizarre mental events.

The mental struggles with life in psychoanalysis and the physical behaviors of animals as a function of specific predictive variables each became its own universe, and psychology was split both ideologically and professionally. The behaviorists claimed a corner on science in their elaborate laboratories of animal learning, for Freudian therapy was hardly rigorous in terms of the canons of science. The Freudians claimed relevance to life as experienced by real people, for behavioristic findings were rarely of direct use even in education, where their central phenomenon, "learning," is crucial.

In one sense, this was objective science versus subjective experience all over again. In behaviorism, the methods of science, measurement, and statistics, were adapted to the exploration of learning, whereas in psychoanalysis, the passions of neurosis were explored with none of the many confounding variables controlled. Each eyed the other with deep suspicion. This polarized thinking left little place for Gestalt, which became marginalized by it.

PSYCHOANALYSIS

Psychoanalysis is both a theory and a treatment strategy. In its treatment component, psychoanalysis has been largely limited in this country to psychiatrists (even though Freud did not believe it should be), but in its theoretical presence, Freud's thought has been a looming presence in psychology as well.[13] Unlike Jung, whose language rarely leaves the mental sphere, or Adler, whose language becomes social but rarely bodily, Freud's invention of psychoanalysis was solidly within a European, physicalistic, medical tradition, and his own training in neurology predisposed him to sit astride the dualistic heritage all must negotiate.

In his earlier theoretical efforts, Freud opted clearly for a model of the mind that imitated physical systems as they were then known.

Looming large in this theory was the concept of energy, *libido*, a concept that refers to no measured quantity but whose quantitative nature made it possible to imitate the precision of science, at least conceptually. Libido was conceived as ultimately biological in origin, and its organization is indebted to Darwinian evolution, such that instincts of *sex* and *aggression*, which facilitate survival in Darwin's world, are the energic legacy of natural selection.

These instinctual forces were represented in the economic model (i.e., the quantitative model) as quanta of energy that drive the organism to behave, and to some extent to behave in such and such a way. I must say "to some extent" because these two instincts have little behavioral specificity; they have instead goals. Hence, any activity that helps the individual to survive competition with his or her planet mates is a form of aggression, and any activity that helps the individual to reproduce is a form of the sex drive. Indeed, these "instincts," which energize the human mind with desire and urge, really name "functions" more than activities or experiences. Functional language, which is discussed later, offers a vocabulary of human behavior that is not beholden to the limits of either the mental realm of ideas and meanings, or the physical realm of structures and mechanics.

A quantum of libidinal energy in the "psychic apparatus" becomes for Freud a "wish"—executing the metaphysical switch from physical to mental, and laying groundwork for the double bookkeeping necessitated by our dualistic heritage. But the larger vocabulary of Freudian theory, although never giving up its roots in either physics or phenomenology, is functional. Repression, attachment, projection, defense—all that individuals do psychologically—are functions. They can be drawn in the diagram of the psychic apparatus, or they can be identified in the stream of consciousness, but their more systematic meaning is of a function within a functional system of organic, and ultimately human, adaptation.

As the century progressed through the depression of the 1930s and the war of the 1940s, psychoanalysis became a much larger part of the language of psychiatry, eclipsed in that profession only by the biological thinking inspired by the advent of psychopharmacology, and then only in the 1960s. By 1970, the biological reductionists were progressively in charge and have remained so. Psychology, with a much richer history of theory than psychiatry, at least in the twentieth century, also became increasingly reductive and biological by the century's end, but always against the backdrop of academic arguments of all kinds, which continue.

It is psychology's great intellectual advantage not to be a part of the profession of medicine. It thus has been liberated from the ethos of both healing and profit-making. At the same time, however, this fact has limited the power of the profession of psychology largely to the academic world, even though there are more clinical psychologists than any other kind.

THE COGNITIVE REVOLUTION

A fourth effort of psychology to deal successfully with the mind–body problem appeared with the "cognitive revolution" in the 1950s and 1960s. This revolution opened a new avenue for U.S. psychology within which scientific studies of thinking, remembering, perceiving, and so on, were possible. It was not begun with a seminal hypothesis about the connection between the mental world and the physical world, as was true in both psychophysics and in Gestalt psychology. Rather, it was inspired largely by the Swiss researcher of children's thinking, Jean Piaget, whose theory about the mental life of the child opened a new vista for psychological science.[14]

Of course, mental life had appeared in the work of psychophysics and Gestalt, and also by this time in the popularity of Freud. But each of these offered complexity and subtlety that yielded not only puzzlement but also contempt—because such work was difficult to pursue scientifically. Thus, when Piaget's theory lent itself to scientific verification, in America and hence globally, it was the sign of real and legitimate knowledge. This was not the first but it was certainly the most sensational application of science to mental life. It did not bridge mental and physical conceptually, as had been attempted by psychophysics or by Gestalt, nor did it relate mental experiences to brain events. Instead, Piaget was undoubtedly interested in the *mental* life of the child, and how it develops. He also theorized about the biological (evolutionary) background of intelligence, but these larger theoretical explorations rarely became important in this country.

It was Piaget's theories of stages of cognitive development that hit U.S. universities in the late 1950s, and have been the scene of enormous progress in the understanding of one's own subjective experiences ever since. The research into the development of cognition in children now seems obvious, but at the time, it was not so, and its practice proved revolutionary. The key link between mental life and the scientific method lay in behavior. How one sees something, and gives it meaning, will determine one's behavior with respect to it. It is difficult to measure accurately one's seeing; it is much less challenging to measure one's behavior.

A child who does not have the intellectual capability to grasp the conservation of volume will prefer to drink his or her juice from a tall thin glass instead of a short fat one because the child thinks there is more juice in the tall one. At a certain age, the child is no longer deceived by such appearances; his or her experience is informed by a knowledge of volume in three-dimensional space. This is but a sample of human discovery made in the development of every life, according to developmental patterns that enable researchers to see just what and how children think . . . and remember, and anticipate, and behave.

Hence, American psychology underwent a "revolution," so that logic and thinking became objects of science. American psychology has been greatly enriched conceptually by taking cognition seriously, and this revolution has most dramatically demonstrated the applicability of science to mental life. But it has made no progress on the underlying problem of dualism. Consequently, the research in cognition, as successful as it is, proceeds primarily by applying the language of physics to the sciences of thinking, remembering, perceiving, and so on.

Scientific logic, and the order of natural events, can supply everyday life with new developmental meaning. Development of thinking, moral maturity, conceptual sophistication, or even perhaps mental health can be explored in this way. This has expanded psychology's range impressively. Thoughts do have frequency, and memory does have accuracy, about which quantitative research can be done. The concrete life of any single individual is not significant because of such quantities, but Piaget brought logic into the purview of the scientific study of the mind. Here again it is obvious that psychology has not forgotten the "psyche" after which it is named. It has turned back on itself in this century as it had tried, less successfully, to do in the nineteenth-century study of psychophysics.

Beyond cognitive science that takes logic as its standard and studies deviations, there are many features of cognition that are neither logical nor illogical, but that produce large differences in how a person behaves. For example, "attributions" of causal efficacy or of personal intentions in the behavior of others determine how one responds to them. A family that has agreed to attribute to its wayward son a willful rejection of guidance will behave in ways that perpetuate the behavior that upsets family members. Parents who blame themselves will create a different atmosphere, and yet a third possibility (among many possibilities) is when parents attribute their child's misbehavior to struggles with the difficulties of forming an identity within the chaos of the modern age. What powers and sensitivities they attribute to the child will shape their behavior, and so such attributions are of immediate clinical relevance.[15]

Attributions are also subject to experimental manipulation, so that psychologists may in time develop useful theory about the conditions under which certain family cultures may be favorable environments for behavior problems. At the same time, however, it is important to note that even the cognitive revolution has yet to transcend the language of quantitative science to explore the multifarious layers of meaning of which subjective experience is made.

It is obvious that in the cognitive revolution, psychological science has come to investigate things previously closed to its methods. Scientifically established theories about families and school rooms and other social settings may in time enable individuals to be less surprised at behaviors they do not understand well. But, although these studies demonstrate that the language of science can apply to behavioral science, they have had a smaller effect in clarifying clinical phenomena.

The "cognitive therapies" of Aaron Beck and others have entered the clinical world and established another kind of psychotherapy that has proven its usefulness.[16] But to explore how a scientific object like the brain is related to cognitions, and thus to perception of one's child, and thus to behavior, remains a barely broached frontier. Psychopharmacological theory has no cognitive content. There has been no additional conceptual clarity at the level of metaphysical dualism. As far as the issues of "cognitive psychology" are concerned, there is no need for a brain–mind resolution, for cognition as it can be studied scientifically is mental, not physical or neurological.

PSYCHOSOMATIC MEDICINE

Human beings sometimes present clinical symptoms of disorder in their bodies that make no medical sense, but that indeed follow a psychological order (Alexander, 1950). Such cases are never simple, but Freud and his followers in the early part of this century were able to speak about mind–body interactions in ways that were then new in the science of medicine. Could it be that a mental conflict, conundrum, or crisis, can be expressed in bodily symptoms without the mind of the individual being aware of such a relation?

Early in his career, Freud struggled with the distinction between "psycho-neuroses" and "actual neuroses"—the former having meaning within the realm of the psyche, the latter being mechanical effects of disease processes in the body, for which the mental counterpart was incidental. Although Freud resisted collapsing all neuroses into psychoneuroses, the term *psychosomatic disease* has suggested that psychological conflicts may well come to be expressed in "body language"—the language of bodily symptoms. Put another way, a psychic conflict, according to Freud, may have various manifestations, from psychological ones like phobias and obsessions, to bodily ones like abdominal pains and muscle weakness.[17]

Obvious here at once is Freud's dualism, for these symptoms were of different groups, mental and physical, and at the same time, his effort to overcome such dualism by citing a common origin is clear. Even sexual impulses, a common culprit in the generation of conflict, are both organic enervations as well as experienced desires. In addition to mental conflicts causing physical ailments, Freud (1905) also noted that positive relationships have healthful outcomes. This idea anticipates current findings in immunology, the latest center of psychosomatic science.

Another key aspect of the effort to negotiate the gap between body and mind appears in the research on alexithymia (Krystal, 1982). *Alexithymia* is the term psychologists give to the inability by some people to name their emotions. First, emotions are usually experienced simultaneously in three ways. They are experienced as events in one's body, such as a pounding heart, shortness of breath, or rush of excitation. Second, emotions are experiences that have names like "anger" and "fear," and such experiences are clearly mental as well as bodily, although there has been an awareness of the closeness of these two since William James. Third, emotions come along with engagements or observations of the environment, such as fear and high places.

Alexithymic individuals seem to have developed a way of experiencing that omits or greatly reduces the second of these three, the conscious recognition, and the verbal name, of the emotion. This experiential and cognitive-naming deficiency makes such individuals less conversant than others with "emotional" events provoked by the environment. Such persons recognize events, and they see corresponding bodily events, but the "emotion" that connects these two is missing, or is unclear and confused.

Failing to take advantage of the experiential signals of felt emotions, and also therefore deficient in the cognitive coping with such emotions, alexithymic individuals' experience themselves as somehow "on another wave length," or even "out of it" socially. Not feeling their anger, for example, they are unable to tell themselves they are angry, or to wonder why, or plan what to do, and so on. Meanwhile, bodily arousal seems to them to be unconnected to either felt emotions or cognitive coping with situations in the environment; thus they feel that their body does what it does in ways beyond their understanding. It seems out of control. They feel mysteriously sick.

Feeling sick leads to announcing oneself as a member of the category "sick person," which in turn, in schools and homes everywhere, alerts others to treat the individual as if he or she is sick. The rewards of such an act make it attractive in itself, but beyond that, being in the sick role also makes comprehensible to people why they are somehow out of touch with what others find and respond to in the environment.

Nemiah and Sifneos (1970) found that psychosomatic patients often could not describe their feelings, nor did they have an ordinary fantasy life within which they rehearsed emotionally charged events, imagining various paths of action and outcomes. This striking lack of imagery corresponded to findings in France by Marty, de M'Uzan, (1974) and David (1963) that many physically ill psychotherapy patients could not describe such fantasies. Both current immunological work and the complex developmental understanding of alexithymia give psychology much more sophisticated directions than the original list of "psychosomatic illnesses": asthma, ulcer, arthritis, headache, hypertension, and pulmonary heart disease.

PSYCHOPHARMACOLOGY

Since 1955, when chlorpromazine (Thorazine) was first introduced in the United States for the treatment of schizophrenia, a sixth real opportunity (and obligation) to bridge the mind–body gap in theory presented itself. This technology, it should be noted, is only the latest investigation of physical treatments of mental disorders, as opposed to the mental causes of physical disorders that were studied in psychosomatic medicine. Drugs followed lobotomy, electroshock, insulin shock, hydrotherapy, and a gruesome catalog of other hunches and extravagances that has been tried historically (cf. Valenstein, 1986).

Only a minority of mental scientists look beyond the practical utility of drugs as a way to handle patients, or to aid patients in handling themselves. Such scientists strive to negotiate between the modern two specialized ways, mental and physical, of experiencing human reality. James Grotstein (1996) is an exemplar of this group. He is a psychoanalyst, a Freudian. Although Freud's theory is very much out of style in the "decade of the brain," Freud's framework serves well if one hopes to continue to take seriously that part of human experience not amenable to exploration by modern physical science.

One useful feature of psychoanalytic language is that it partakes of multiple discourses at once. On the mental side are terms like *desire* and *anxiety*, which name specific mental experiences, and on the other side lies *libido*, a metaphorical energy, never used to name a reality as much as to evoke a quantitative and mechanical, physical and causal framework within which the science of things flourishes. Freud, like others, never offered a modulus of translation between a qualitative desire and a quantitative "energy," between the stuff of mental and physical worlds, but he did develop a language that lay between these two dualistically divided discourses.

Freud offered a language of "function," which describes more than the physical machinery by explaining what it does. The doing follows organismic patterns but also mental ones, without naming, as mental discourse does, spiritual realities like desire. A cathexis is a hypothetical organization of energy dynamics in an energy distributing system ("the mental apparatus") that orients the person to the world in ways one names mentally as love, danger, loss—the content of human experience.

Grotstein is an analyst, interested in that most difficult of mental illnesses, schizophrenia.[18] He also knew that the physical (pharmacological) treatment of mental disorders was promising, and probably here to stay. He, therefore, attempted to work out "how psychoanalysis must modify its theories and techniques generally and specifically, and what lessons neurobiology can learn from psychoanalysis" (p. 1).

On the mental side, Grotstein knew that any description of any disorder must deal in the currency of development. The brain is enormously plastic and so its development and that of the mental organization of one's being in the world develop together. These are the same development, of course, and yet the two languages are incommensurate. For example, a memory is almost certainly represented in the physical brain in some fashion, but there is little concrete idea how. At the same time, remembering a terrifying experience in a relationship can alter an individual's willingness to trust or risk anything in a future relationship. And yet after a few weeks on Prozac, the individual may find him or herself able to take risks heretofore impossible.

Can it then be said that the mental effects of Prozac are known? Not really, for such effects are not always the same. If the individual can imagine him or herself being different, he or she may struggle to overcome his or her inhibitions, and the individual may garner the courage to try. Is Prozac a drug of courage? Surely it is not this simple. The individual may in fact have done something *new* in his or her experience, but he or she cannot say what exactly that is, so the effects of Prozac cannot thus be labeled psychologically.

Grotstein was quite interested in human relationships, and he viewed their crucial role in the development of one's entire life. But in the case of a schizophrenic, Grotstein argued that a "relationship" may be a new thing. Relationships are rare for schizophrenics, he believes, because they violate an earlier decision by schizophrenics—a "Faustian bargain" that he described in their development. The person seems to have purchased "the illusion of safety at the expense of "going-on-being" (p. 10)—a bargain "that forecloses on the pursuit of pleasure and of playing in life" (p. 2) so that at best the individual can only observe him or herself trying to play, or to trust, or to live—all the time knowing that the effort itself has been surrendered and the result is nothing more than "the inexorable feeling of being a fraud" (p. 2).

This experience is at once a contemporary subjective state of affairs and a vaguely sensed memory. It is impossible to describe "trusting" or "pursuit of pleasure" or "being a fraud" in neuropharmacological terms, and yet such chemical language is the language of the most powerful treatments of schizophrenia. "Eventually, a sobering consensus seems to have developed between the use of psychotropics for the treatment of disorganizing *states* and psychotherapy for the residual personality *traits*" (p. 3). These terms, *states* and *traits*, both refer to mental and physical realms. Both are perhaps examples of "embodied mind and will" (Fell, personal communication, 1997). A state is relatively temporary and a trait is more enduring, but as a division of labor between professions and approaches, it offers little more than and abstract bridge across the mind–body divide.

Perhaps more fruitful is the language of information processing. Grotstein cited many studies about the schizophrenic's "inability to sustain an intentional focus of attention" (Anscombe, 1987), "deficiency of working memory" (Goldman-Rakic, 1993), "impairment of willed action" (Frith, 1989), and "a deficiency in processing and integrating information" (Knight & Fischer, 1992), to mention only a few. With such language, comes a focus on neither mechanical/causal nor subjective/experiential language, but a kind of functional language that reminds us that Freud, along with Robert Woodworth and William James, saw this possibility, and its importance, a century ago.

FUNCTIONAL LANGUAGE

Functional language is not all alike. Some terms are closer to the discourse of bodily causality, whereas others are closer to the discourse of mind and experience. Within functional language, therefore, it may be useful to envision a continuum of concepts anchored at one end in scientific language and, at the other, in experiential language. Some terms are, in other words, more "corporo-tropic," whereas others are more "ideo-tropic." Mining Grotstein's (1996) summary essay entitled "Orphans of the 'Real': Some Modern and Postmodern Perspectives on the Neurobiological and Psychosocial Dimensions of Psychosis and Other Primitive Mental Disorders," one may observe such a range of functional terms.

An exemplary corporo-tropic functional term is *neural integration*—as in the sentence by Feinberg (1987): "A defect in this (presumably) genetically controlled process might impair mechanisms of neural integration and thereby produce the illness in at least a subgroup of patients within the schizophrenic syndrome" (p. 507). Neural integration is a physical arrangement of nerves and neural bundles in which larger units of neural functioning are woven together to handle certain combinations of sensory, motivational, and cognitive content, each of which is a "mechanism" that serves the larger, integrated functional unit.

An exemplary ideo-tropic functional term is *impairment of willed action* (Frith, 1989). Between neural integration and impairment of willed action lay such ideas as defective gating of sensory data, information processing, language disorder, defective orienting response, deficiency in working memory—all naming functions that function badly in the presence of (as symptoms of) schizophrenia.

RESOLUTION?

No, psychology and psychiatry are a long way from the modulus that would connect mental language and neurological (physical) language. But functional language is, at once, about physical structures in the sense of saying what they do, and it is about human experience as well, naming abstractly categories of what experiences do.

In the effort to undercut dualism by pointing to the new descriptive beginning by Miller and by Merleau-Ponty, it can be seen that an individual is an embodied will, a material consciousness, the elements of which have been divided for centuries into mind and body to limited good effect. Fell pointed out that theory might begin again with the "act," an event that is physical because it, like one's mind, is embodied, and yet follows patterns more akin to the order of ideas and its "freedom" than to the causality of the order of natural events. This also accords with the suggestion of another philosopher, Steven Pepper (1942). Acts are intended by an actor, but intentions too can be seen functionally. May functionalism offer a way out, finally, of dualism?

NOTES

1. The noteworthy exception to this generalization is the literature of the philosophy of science, which deals with knowing largely in terms of logic, a traditional but quite specialized focus of philosophy.

2. The solution to the mind–body problem was not the only seemingly urgent task of scientific psychology. Additionally, the related but separable problem of veridicality in perception made all scientific perception subject first to correction by the science of psychology. Psychology was called, therefore, by Boring (1950) the "propaedeutic science," the preliminary and preparatory science. Such breakthroughs as Helmholz's measurement, in 1850, of neural transmission in the human body, for example, promised such corrective action by knowers limited by their psychophysical apparatus.

3. I am skipping over Wilhelm Wundt in this account, whose laboratory in Leipzig pioneered much of this work. Boring (1950) explained that Wundt called his work "physiological psychology" as a reference to the two roots of his science, the chronologically first in British empiricist philosophers who worked analytically within the mental realm, and dating back to the ancient Greeks, and the second in the scientific breakthroughs in the earlier nineteenth century, such as Helmholz's measurement of neural trans-

mission. From the philosophers, Wundt adopted the subject matter of the mind; from the scientists, Wundt adopted the methods of their science. To champion this approach, which is still current in psychology, was to go against the notion of mind as "transcendent" of such methods, a notion shared by Kant, Fichte, Schelling, and others. Such a view is still often called *metaphysical*, which also expresses a muted contempt for philosophy entertained by scientists who believe that only science yields real knowledge.

Wundt himself was not as sure that his methods could provide final knowledge, for higher mental processes, in his view, would only be resolved in his *Volkerspsychologie* (social psychology), which was to be something like a history of human knowing. This contrasts with a more Kantian view by Brantano, who did not share Wundt's faith that science can proceed independently of (uncolored by) metaphysical assumptions. Ironically, no one studies Brentano today, but his central concept of "intentionality" is as important and problematic—and prescient—today as it has always been, to both scholars and lay persons, although they rarely acknowledge it.

4. James had enormous respect for research and theory, but about the introspective methods of psychophysics practiced by Wundt and Titchener, he avered that, for his part, he would rather classify all the pebbles and stones on a New Hampshire hillside than undertake their kind of laboratory work.

5. Watson's *Behaviorism*, first published in 1924, became the flag of victory in positive science's bid to define knowledge in psychology. Simplistic by modern standards, and having none of the subtlety of James before him or Gestalt psychologists after him, Watson's work nevertheless energized several decades of scientific research, and laid the ground work for contemporary scientific psychology.

6. While psychologists wanted psychology to be a science, all successful scientific methods applied to the mind lead to little accumulation of useful data. No wonder, of course, for science assumes that "reality" has the stability and repeatability of the material world. Watson's omission of mental life from U.S. psychology may therefore have seemed necessary at the time, but it badly constrained the science. Fortunately, his dogmatic reject of mental life as subject matter was surpassed by mid-century.

7. E. C. Tolman's most seminal book was *Purposive Behavior in Animals and Men*, first published in 1932 by the Century Company. Tolman stubbornly held out for "mentalistic" language as descriptors of even rat behavior, and he legitimated the "hypothetical construct" as a metatheoretical justification that has withheld the test of time.

8. Watson was aggressively uncompromising, describing any notion of "mind" as a mere perpetuation of "metaphysics" (as opposed to science), religious beliefs (as opposed to science) and other "heritages of a timid savage past" (p. 3).

9. I have not included an extended discussion of behaviorism in this survey of psychology's struggle with dualism, but I must note that Watson was adamantly a physicalist, rejecting mental life entirely as the subject matter of psychology. The vehemence of this rejection does suggest an intense struggle, felt acutely by Watson, but also by most of psychology in the early decades of this century. More than anything, psychologists wanted psychology to be a science, but nearly all scientific method successfully applied to the mind failed to lead to an accumulation of useful data.

Behavior, conceived as physical movement in physical space, did not have that problem. To define psychology as the "science of behavior" does exploit much of the stability and repeatability of the material world—features notably absent from so much of mental life. Watson's "solution" was radical surgery that ablated all of consciousness from psychology, and it gave up too much. In those early decades, human psychology progressed either by being courageously non-Watsonian or by studying animals, whose mental life was of interest, but whose historical import was not their "minds." Rather, animal psychology was pivotal in the joining of the methods of experimental science to the study of behavior, which could be seen as indicating "the mind." However, the science of behavior often was simply that—about behavior, and not about the mind at all. Thus the hegemony of behaviorism was a somewhat distant but also an important chapter in psychology's struggle with dualism.

10. Much of this work has spun off from Pavlov, as did Watson's original theory. Pavlovian work has, of course, been a staple for psychology for the entire twentieth century. Other learning theorists have also been important, studying behavior rather than glandular responses, eventuating in Skinner, whose behaviorism theory is equally provocative, being notably broader in application than those of either Pavlov or Watson, while retaining a positivist definition of scientific knowledge.

11. Of all the published theoretical work in Gestalt psychology, the most accessible, even to psychologists, is Koehler (1947).

12. The reasons are not exactly mysterious; they are understood in terms of the historical choices made by Watson and others to declare the methods of physical science to be adequate to and necessary for real knowledge in the emerging science of psychology. What is mysterious is not what happened in this development of science, nor even why it happened. What is

mysterious is how to change it, how to equate, or translate, or correlate, those phenomena formulated in physical terms with those experienced mentally by everyone.

13. I believe that Freud's *Collected Papers*, translated by Joan Riviere, is the most useful single collection of Freud's work. It does not include major and long works by Freud, which are usually accessible by title, but the selection offers much that is readable to the layperson, even though the papers are often specialized. It was published in the United States by Basic Books in 1959. It is tempting to say more about the gigantic accomplishment of Freud by suggesting the size of the bridge that would connect, say, Darwin and Erikson. Both are "modern," but Freud's modernity is much more central to our transition into the "post-modern" than is Darwin's. Note that the entire field of psychosomatic medicine (Alexander, 1950) would be impossible without Freudian thought.

14. I recommend Piaget (1955), *The Language and Thought of the Child*, as a typical sample of Piaget's elaborate observational style and theoretical constructions. Piaget's ability to bridge the temporal gap between the early twentieth-century educational psychology of Thorndike and the practical concerns of the twenty-first-century classroom indicates something of the importance of this thinker in the history of psychology.

15. It is also important that attributions have come to play an important role in social psychology, for phenomena like prejudice, for example, yield to conceptual analysis of how we attribute motives and traits to individuals and groups, which in turn brings the wealth of experimental data in attribution theory to bear on social problems.

16. Beck's (1967) extension of cognitive psychology into the clinical field is best described in *Depression: Clinical, Experimental, and Theoretical Aspects*.

17. See Volume 1 of the *Collected Papers* (Freud, 1959).

18. See also Sarbin & Juhasz (1982) for an excellent review of the history of the concept, "schizophrenia, and its complex interaction with both the experience so named and the often unkind reaction to that experience and its experiencer."

chapter 4

ON BIOLOGICAL REDUCTIONISM

Culture and Ideology

CAUSAL FACTORS IN PSYCHOPATHOLOGY

In considering the antecedent factors in the creation of those personal problems called *psychopathology*, one needs to take account of the following:

1. Biological variables such as genetics and hormonal/neurochemical factors.
2. Experiential interpretations of present, past, and future events.
3. The events themselves as they are evaluated at a social or cultural level.

Very good books, such as Preston, O'Neal, and Talaga's (1997) *Handbook of Clinical Pharmacology for Therapists*, bias our understanding, unwittingly, I am sure. In a time of hegemony, very visible and popular leadership, domination even, by a particular point of view, becomes an ideology and constitutes a bias. Such biases are the stuff of which is made scientific failure. For example, in the late 1990s, biological psychiatry dominated all competitors. The effect of this

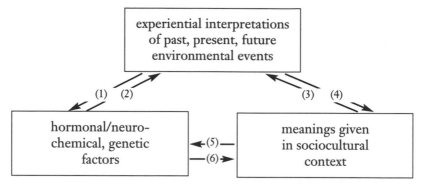

FIG. 4.1.   *Factors and Their Relationships in Psychopathology.*[1]

domination can be seen in a careful analysis of professional writing, even very good, very competent, professional writing.

If the combination of causal factors includes a biological one, the current ideology in science will lead to privileging that one focus for understanding causes and for prescribing treatment. A look at these factors and their likely or established relations will demonstrate this point. Although causality is always complex, the fairly simple diagram may help to illustrate the point (see Fig. 4.1).

Preston et al. (1997) made quite clear that there are "many studies and clinical findings that collectively provide strong support for the idea that environmental and psychological factors can significantly affect biological and neurological functioning" (p. 19). This is Connection 1. Environmental events affect brain functioning in the short run quite noncontroversially, and plausibly in the longer run as well, so that repeated experiences of environmentally caused sadness may yield more or less permanent biological changes. These changed brain functions can in turn affect psychological experience, which is Connection 2 and which is another notion beyond controversy.

One's experience of events is also shaped by meanings that are given from the cultural context, which is Connection 3. However, the relevant meanings from that context are themselves the result of experiences by persons. Beyond that, exactly which meanings from the larger culture will be accepted result from the filtering and selecting by one's experiential categories, so that individuals also psychologically determine the way the culture will affect them. This selection and filtering gets re-enacted in the culture itself, which is Connection 4. Finally, different cultures produce different patterns of recognition and reaction that are, over developmental time in a given culture, represented in neural organizations. This is Connection 5, and yet these neural patterns, once organized, select what experiences from the culture will be allowed to register in the patterns of brain chemistry, and these patterns feed back into the culture as well. This is Connection 6, which says that having been brought up an American, for example, I now filter the impact of meanings of my experiences in Japan in such a way that many Japanese meanings escape me. Were I to live in Japan, I would (in a small way) influence that culture with my neural patterns.

This causal matrix becomes simplified in various literatures, and every simplification privileges one or another factor. Preston et al (1997) did this by beginning with a biologically based depression caused by antihypertensive drugs, prescribed to reduce a patient's blood pressure. These drugs "have an impact on the individual's sense of self-worth and competency in the world. Conversely, this increased level of despair can, in itself, operate to intensify the underlying biological abnormality" (p. 20). Both blood pressure and brain chemistry can be affected. What these authors did not say is that the underlying problem could originally have been psychological or cultural, and that its effect on the biological factors could intensify the underlying psychological problem or cultural problem.

Therefore, to dwell on the case of a biologically caused depression and its usual effects on the other factors, is to focus attention on one of a variety of etiologic pictures. Furthermore, to draw attention to the feedback from other factors so that they make the biological disorder worse is to put the biological disorder into the center. There is no logical or empirical reason not to focus on the possibility that the originating factor was a psychological one, such as rejection or failure, which caused changes in both the brain organization and the person's eventual effect on the culture. Both of these can well feed back to the person's experiential life to make the underlying psychological problem worse.

The partiality in the theorizing by Preston et al. is partly because the book is about psychopharmacology, which is relevant to changing the biological component of the entire picture. Hence, it is an obvious focus for their discussion. But I must nevertheless conclude that authors such as these, who are unusually careful, will likely or inevitably perpetuate impressions that conform to biological centrality, and thus perpetuate a narrowness in theory and practice, whether they intend to or not.

Indeed, looking again at Fig. 4.1, it is revealed that each of these three factors names possible origins of psychopathology, and also that a change in any one of them could and perhaps usually does eventuate in corresponding changes in all three. Furthermore, there is a holistic coherence to human behavior that the diagram restores after the coherence of behavior has been arbitrarily divided up among three separate disciplines. Hence, the diagram is about conceptually separable factors, but not necessarily actually separate factors, in the cause of psychopathology. It is also about separate modes of therapeutic change, which may or may not be combined.

However, it makes a big difference to a depressed person, where one locates the problem. Is the problem *in* the individual's biology, or *in* his or her mental, experiential life, or *in* the culture? It may be in all three by the time the case comes to the attention of a practitioner, but this "where" may or may not be systematically sought. Where it is sought in any particular case will be determined largely by the tradition and ideology within which the practitioner is working. And from this location of the problem by the practitioner, say, in the biology of the person, it follows that the treatment would be biological (pharmacological, usually, or, in the case of Seasonal Affective Disorder, which is treated by the administration of more light, photological).

For this reason, the perhaps excusably incomplete description by Preston et al. becomes a case in ideological transmission, and further, it deals with an ideology that has consequences for the training of professionals, for the legal codification of disorders, for the indexing that triggers insurance payments, and most of all, for the way people in general come to understand their own distress.[2]

The import of reductionism, therefore, is not merely theoretical. In psychiatry, the centering of attention on biological and neurological events radically changes psychiatric treatment. Rarely has such a theoretical shift inspired such an immediate shift in practice, and one should seek to understand the relation between the theoretical and practical changes.

In the actual, historical development of psychiatry's adoption of pharmacology as its main therapeutic technique, one can say the practice affected the theory, but this effect is also embedded in an *interaction* with how theory and practice affected one another. Researchers began to think (again) biologically about "mental illness" in a major way with the discovery in the 1950s that pills sometimes actually work. Even though there were side-effects and other imperfections, and even though the earlier radical departures from mere hospitalization (e.g., lobotomy) had failed dismally, this partial success looked more than promising. Furthermore, the existence of side effects pointed to work yet to do within a biological framework. In no way did side-effects or other imperfections of drug treatment negate the flourishing biological theory that psychosis is a brain disease.[3]

However, examining Fig. 4.1 again, practice and theory both filter back into the causes of the distress that bring clients to treatment. All three of the causal factors in the diagram are affected by theory and practice of prescribing medication. Of course, the most immediate impact of prescribing drugs is the change in brain chemistry. This change then affects the client's experience as inevitably, if not as immediately. More remotely, but also seen eventually and powerfully, these changes in brain chemistry and personal experience have profound impacts on cultural meanings, the meanings given to feeling distressed, or witnessing distress, or seeking help, or following faithfully the doctor's orders. Hence, we see practice, theory, brain chemistry, personal experiences, and cultural meanings, all turning on one gigantic wheel of professional change from the first to the second half of the twentieth century.

It may now be concluded that biological reductionism, a theoretical shift that has happened in history a number of times, became in this, as in previous centuries, part of a change not only of treatment, but of all these things. Most importantly, such a shift eventually produces changes in other conditions that are thought to have a role in the creation of what we call mental illness. Therefore, we need to assess biological reductionism in terms of broader public, professional, legal, and institutional terms, as well as in terms of ideas and ideologies. Biological reductionism is part of a change that changes everything important in our understanding of the creation of mental illness, with the exception of the possible role of the gene pool. In its final manifestation, then, biological reductionism is a cultural event.

This is not the first time that a change in theory and practice has affected the conditions that create illness. The discovery of bacterial and viral infections in the production of illnesses changed definitions of illness, theories, practices, and also people's understanding of their suffering, both personally and at a general cultural level. However, there is a telling difference in the present case of mental illness; changing brain chemistry changes all these things much faster than did the progressive adaptation of institutional practices to such earlier discoveries in medicine.

The more widespread is the actual change of one's brain in this way—the more people's minds are in fact shaped by chemicals—the less critical the assessment of all these movements. Although fewer than the entire population is on drugs, U.S. consumers do tend to trust the expertise of doctors. The readiness of doctors to prescribe psychiatric medications results partly from the fact that the drugs often work well enough to prevent recurrent unproductive visits. Doctors can, in this way, come to depend on drugs as much as their patients.

This dependency among professionals on psychopharmacology is not a chemical addiction. Its dynamics are more complex, involving professional and cultural factors such as how treatment is financed, what the public expects, and how professionals need to behave in order to ensure their personal and professional positions. In other words, nothing short of a sociocultural–political–economic analysis will account for the rapidly advancing hegemony of psychopharmacology.

IS THIS A PROFESSIONAL CRISIS?

The issue is biological reductionism. It is largely a theoretical matter, although its consequences are widespread. This choice or preference is in the hands of professionals. Much of the experience that might indicate that this choice is questionable is in the hands of patients. The traditional practice, when medications do not seem to do what is expected of them, is to try different medicines, or different combinations. Sometimes, doctors decide early on that chemicals are not helpful, but this is neither routine nor typical.

There then might appear a controversy about psychotropic drugs as a professional crisis—in the literal sense of "crossroads." At crossroads, a choice must be made. The argument here about the crisis is not that the choice is being evaded; the argument here is that the choice is being made without enough careful consideration. Reading the psychiatric literature, one can see, in the late 1960s and through the 1970s, the professional consciousness of a *choice* disappear behind a kind of *assumption* that pharmacology is the future of psychiatry (Keen, 1998).

Some may support this assumption by pointing out, as this analysis does, the interrelation of the various causal factors I have described. Presumably, intervening at any point will eventually affect each factor in the matrix of causes. One might come to the conclusion that it does not matter where one begins. Because everything is interrelated, any intervention finally affects all the factors.

It is important to answer this argument, because doctors need a reason to not believe that breaking the chain of causality can happen equally well at any point. This belief is clearly wrong. Depression, when it is a symptom of something wrong in the culture, or in my experience, is a signal that one should pay attention to the fact that something is wrong. Indeed, one may need to see clearly what is wrong in the culture or in one's experience, and seek ways to change it. To let the pharmacological process solve the problem of an individual's depression would be analogous to canceling out pain when the pain is announcing a very different problem that needs attention. Ultimately, it could even be like letting painkillers erase the motivation to operate when an operation is necessary.

Another reason professionals may minimize the crisis character of the changes wrought by biological reductionism is the faith, often enough unjustified, that the self-correcting character of normal science will prevent a major error from occurring. This may be true, at the level of theory, if psychologists, who pay attention to psychological rather than to biological facts, are alert enough to note the rather strained character of published defenses of biological reductionism, or, more rarely, to the ideological factor that merely presumes but does not argue that it all starts with biological facts. The work by Ross and Pam (1995) is an example of such psychological vigilance.

At the level of practice, however, when a drug changes one's experience, this treatment may eliminate the feedback in the life of the person suffering from experiential or sociocultural causes of suffering. The consciousness-changing character of the treatment can prevent the recognition that the causal problem remains, or even that it continues to get worse. If a client can eliminate his or her depression chemically, he or she can hold out indefinitely against recognizing that he or she has marital problems, or that he or she should change jobs. Even more likely, any political or cultural policies that are depressing the patient would be masked by his or her chemically induced feeling of all being right with the world.

IS THIS A PHILOSOPHICAL CRISIS?

Biological reductionism is a theory and a practice, and it affects one's brain chemistry, one's experience, and eventually it affects the cultural frames within which these matter. But biological reductionism is also a shortcut solution to a philosophical problem, often formulated as mind–body dualism. Meanings from the culture, like the experiences in my life, are "mental," do not occupy space, nor have they material size and shape. Brain chemistry, in contrast, is "physical," does occur in space and has the kind of material presence of all objects of biological science.

The language of mental life is moral, as well as rational; expressive as well as calculative. Its format tends to deal with a tension between standards of "good" and "rational," on the one hand, and temptation and emotion, as well as irrationalities in one's beliefs, on the other. That tension is always a space within which persons make choices. The language of mental life assumes human freedom to recognize standards and conform to them, or to ignore and violate them. This realm of experiential life is rich in legend and fantasy and narrative and values, wishes, and tragedies, all of which confront individuals with choices. Human freedom is palpable and central to everyone's lives.

The language of physical events, in contrast, is a language of causality. There are no choices, nor moralities, no range of preference here. What is scientifically true is true because of the order of things and events in nature, their causal, systemic, and molecular features. When A causes B, there is no moral judgment at work. Individuals may have feelings about it in their experience, but that is the other, experiential language. In scientific language, there is no free will. Even what appears unpredictable may very well later turn out to be not random but orderly, when later one has a grasp of the relevant causal pattern of which it is a part.

The suffering of a mental patient is mental; the treatment is physical. The application of scientific causality to the realm of experiential freedom and morality is certainly possible, but to cross that divide is to indulge two incommensurate languages as if their relationship were known. In fact, there is only a seat-of-the-pants grasp of what exactly is being done when mental problems are healed with pills. Practitioners do know that the pills affect brain chemistry, very likely affecting rates of transmission from one cell to another, among certain cells, in certain brain structures. Which structures, however, is known only partially, and the rest is more theory than fact.

But even as theoretical possibilities are replaced with facts, the profession does not make lucid how affecting experience with physical means should be understood in terms of one's moral and rational language. Does changing my experience chemically solve the problem I have in my experience, which is about situations in the world, which I cannot help but understand in terms of choices made possible by the free spaces created in moral and rational discourse?

Furthermore, how problems coded in moral and rational terms (dealing with immoralities and irrationalities) justify physical intervention is not made lucid by advances in research in neurochemistry and physiology. The fact that individuals can change their experience with chemicals is familiar from knowledge of alcohol. It is no accident that the understanding of alcohol is cluttered from top to bottom and edge to edge with moral struggles against temptations, indulgences, escapes, and failures, moral struggles with profits in sales and criminal liabilities. Is this cacophony of controversy somehow different in the question of psychotropic drugs? The case of psychotropic drugs certainly can be more subtle, but in principle, at least some of the moral and rational upheavals of alcohol and other recreational drugs is just as present in the case of psychiatric medicines.

In psychiatry, professional decorum and legal tending mute this cacophony of controversy, based largely on the convenience of calling personal problems "diseases," but that itself is also a magic trick whereby issues in one language conveniently get processed in another. The upheavals of personal terrors and tragedies can be reduced to, and treated within, the language of neurophysiology and chemistry. But the conceptual sleight of hand here returns us to the task of understanding the moral and rational meanings of brain events.

It is my conclusion, of course, that beneath these conceptual gaps and pretenses lay the philosophical problem of the relation between mind and body. Centuries of work by philosophers have not resolved this matter, but there are many fruitful and promising starts. The philosophy of John William Miller, discussed briefly in chapter 2, is an example. In what follows, an effort is made to utilize this start to elucidate the conceptual morass of psychopharmacology. Note how easily that term, *psychopharmacology*, combines body and mind into one, as if merely specifying a subspecialty of pharmacology, like gastric pharmacology or hepatico-pharmacology. That convenience speaks both a truth and a falsehood. The truth is that drugs do affect psyche. The falsehood is the implication that we know what we are doing when we do so.

Bodily language and mental language belong to two vastly different traditions of understanding. Bodily language is the disciplined and precise language of science, and mental language is the complexly layered, multimeaninged, experiential language of everyday life. In earlier chapters, it became clear that these languages are both quite widely applicable in individuals' lives, and that individuals must, in the mere process of living, negotiate differing conclusions to which each language would lead. Free will–determinism, morality–medicine, ideals–inevitabilities—each of these polarities express implicit underlying dualism. Psychopharmacology does not escape this dilemma but in fact enacts it, knowingly (when one sees clearly) or unconsciously (when one does not).

In order to break new ground, researchers will have to rethink human behavior, and the paradigm case will be the experience of taking psychotropic drugs. A man goes to a psychiatrist with symptoms of depression. The psychiatrist notes the symptoms, makes a diagnosis of Major Depressive Disorder and prescribes Prozac, 20 mg, QID. After a few weeks, the patient feels better. In one sense, what happened here is known, but in another it is not. The medical language suffices to place these events into a comprehensible frame, but that language does not include moral issues, nor the complex layers of the patient's life, nor the meanings in his experience. How can this be thought about differently, taking into account what the medical language omits but not giving up what it offers?

DESCRIBING ANEW

A human is an embodied consciousness. He is not a disembodied one, whose life is a struggle with the ideals of rationality and morality, untouched by causality. Nor is he an unconscious body, whose life merely plays out the effects of the many causes that control it. He is a conscious, willful body, ensnared in both of these networks of human life. Culture provides standards against which he measures himself, including standards of well-being and happiness, against which he thinks of himself as "disturbed" or "depressed" or "pathological" somehow. Important people also contribute to this judgment, and his sense of his success and failure, his effort toward goodness, his loyalty and rationality—all have led him to the doctor, for he sees in himself failure, lack of goodness, inconsequential loyalty, and inconsistent rationality. He come to the conclusion that there is something wrong with his life, and that he is not the person he should be.

The processes I have described so far all sound mental, but the patient is excruciatingly aware of how coerced he is by causes that seem beyond his control, such as his promiscuous impulses that compromise his loyalty; his desire every night for alcohol, which he fears may be an addiction; his backache, which seems relentless when everything else goes wrong; and his sense that people generally have just not given him credit for how hard he tries to be the kind of person he should be, or the person someone else wants him to be. He feels trapped in a network of circumstances, some of which he created, of course, but all of which now press in on him without his being able to influence them. The trapped part of his feeling makes him say that *none* of this is his fault. The less frequent realization that the individual himself created some of these conditions leads him to exaggerate and say that it is all his fault. The individual vacillates between sometimes hating himself and more often hating everyone else.

Having described just this much, I have inevitably entered into the great ambivalence in all psychopathology, between blaming oneself and blaming other people and other factors. Insofar as I blame myself, I construe all this within a moral language that gives me free will. Insofar as I am a victim of things beyond my control, I am not the actor but the victim. I may still attribute free will to others, and thus judge their treatment of me, but this moral sense is often dwarfed by the sense that my behavior is caused by others, by my friends and family, by 1,000 circumstances beyond my control.

Now of course this vignette description vastly oversimplifies the experience of a patient. But what a patient is likely to hear from a doctor is even simpler, especially if that doctor is a biological reductionist. The ambivalence ("Who is to blame here, me as moral agent or factors outside that agency?") will be resolved by the professional affirmation of the latter. "You are suffering from a chemical imbalance in the brain, and we now have ways of treating these conditions. Let me write you a prescription for . . .") This kind of talk clearly uses the language of objects and causality. It does not speak to the part of the individual's experience that is free to choose an attitude, a behavior, a course of action, a lifestyle, or a career.

The experience of this particular patient makes an enormous difference for his recovery. The ambivalence with which the patient began at least kept open the possibility that there may be some ways he could decide to handle situations that puzzle or upset him. In what the doctor says, the possibility of taking some initiative on his own behalf is reduced, along with his uncertainty about what is wrong. The prescription tells the patient that he has a disease that is now being treated by the doctor. The only decision the patient must make is to be cjompliant.

The patient might opt to reject the doctor's expertise, or the patient might overcome that temptation because of the realization that he is not doing well on his own. All sorts of traditional clichés urge the patient to comply, as does the assumption of faith in experts. Therefore, the patient buries his own willfullness as misguided arrogance and self-serving overconfidence. Latent throughout such an internal dialogue is the patient's dualism, which pits his sense of freedom against his sense of malleability by objective causes.

In a way, compliance resolves the dualism. Without the expertise of the doctor, the patient would have no ability to help himself. Helping himself here happens only if the patient is helped by someone else. The patient's independence depends on his prior dependency.

The account so far emphasizes the part of the patient's problem that appears to be caused, and correspondingly reduces the part that the patient may freely choose in a space structured by a moral ideal or a rational standard. If this is an error, it is important to note the reciprocal error. Some problems are caused by factors outside the patient's control, and to emphasize what is within his control may be just as self-defeating. A doctor is less likely to make this mistake than a psychotherapist who may assume one's life is one's responsibility—period. However, what both would be unable to do is to help the individual to understand him or herself in both ways at once.

And yet that is the sort of understanding toward which individuals should strive. For humans are neither a body caught up in a flurry of causes, nor a mind that does what it decides independently of causality. Clearly, if the patient takes pills as prescribed, he will still be deciding things, and yet the "I" who is deciding is being intentionally changed by causal agents like chemicals that affect his neurotransmitters, that affect his mind. What pills do is affect his consciousness. If they do not do so, they are not psychotropic medicines. That is their purpose and it is the criteria of their effectiveness.

Fast forward a month and the patient is feeling better. Two side-effects occur. The patient is off again–on again impotent, and he finds he cannot cry. Such side-effects are of course not wanted by either the professionals or the patient. They are called *side-effects* because of the focus on the *main effect*, a term given to the reason why the drug was prescribed in the first place.

Instead of awaiting the pharmaceutical refinement that may accomplish this tighter targeting of drug effects, one should ask whether impotence and crying offer further descriptive possibilities for overcoming dualism. Crying and sexuality reveal vivid cases of human mind–body unity. One's mental experience and one's body are congruent; both express "me," right now, in this situation. That expression not only combines one's mind and body into a person, it is also perceived by others, recognized, acknowledged, and responded to in ways that consolidate its meaning within a cultural matrix of meanings.

Most individuals' lives are like this, unified across the dualistic split and congruent with others' expectations and understanding. One's tears, one's sadness, and someone else's acknowledgment of both are a human experience that not only bridges gaps in mind–body and self–others, but also past–present. The present experience falls into an historically shaped tradition of, say, mourning, or making love. The actual patterns of life are as indebted to history as they are to the cause–effect relations of the body or to struggles for a rational grasp or a good decision within mental life.

However, with mourning and love-making in mind, let us return to the descriptive task. The goal is to focus our thought at a level of life less abstract and detailed than either of the specialized languages we began with. I suggest another example.

If a man were to watch his diet in order eventually to eliminate his craving for sweets or alcohol, he would be deciding mentally to change his physical neural structures and functions in order to change the consciousness within which he decides. Is not taking a drug a decision very like recovering from alcoholism? A decision is necessary. It affects one's brain. This change in the man's brain makes his consciousness, and future decisions, different from before the process started. Or is taking a drug more like becoming an alcoholic, which is a process of deciding mentally to indulge a pleasure that changes one's physical neural structures and functions, which in turn changes the consciousness within which the individual decides?

The only way to discriminate, at this level of theory, between becoming an alcoholic and recovering from alcoholism would be to establish that one consciousness is clearer, more astute, accurate, and precise in dealing with reality, than the other consciousness. In the case of alcoholism, which is clearer depends on how deeply alcoholic one is. After a certain level of dependency is reached, consciousness without alcohol is less astute than after a few drinks. That enhanced astuteness, however, does not allow one to stop drinking. The progress of the binge inevitably shows that alcohol makes even the alcoholic less astute, not more.

Presumably, the case is different with psychotropic drugs. Certain addictionlike properties of benzodiazepines, however, suggest that the difference is subtle. Valium is a very difficult drug to stop taking after some years of moderate use. Mood stabilizers like Tegretol or lithium seem to cut down the variation in moods, but many prefer the variation to the stability. Or is it an astuteness they prefer? Schizophrenics are frequently noncompliant because they find the relative sanity after phenothiazines to be less attractive than the psychotic experiences such drugs cure.[4] Is the attractiveness of the nondrugged state because they are more or because they are less astute? Or interesting, or hedonic, or liberating, or does reality appear more real?

Many patients report, however, that they are better at making decisions after a few weeks on Prozac. It is as if they find their minds less cluttered with what seems to be irrelevant and self-defeating content, such as fantasies of failure or routines of self-protection. This experience is also important. What is not known is whether this change eliminates something that may be important, or whether it would be better to deal with it in terms of its content instead of its inconvenience. Dealing with the content may be an occasion of growth. That possibility is lost along with the "symptom."

The most important discovery, however, in this exploration is that these questions are imponderable to those who prescribe psychotropic medication. They also seem of little interest to people in general insofar as consensus affirms that "medicines" are good and "symptoms" are bad. All of this needs rethinking.

NOTES

1. The tradition of describing many levels of analysis at once is of course a respected one. The most elaborate such effort in psychiatry is Engel (1980).

2. At this point, I offer another example, a book I believe is among the most thoughtful, written for the public instead of for the practitioner, *When Words are not Enough: The Women's Prescription for Depression and Anxiety*, by Valerie Davis Raskin (MD). After recognizing both mental and physiological causality (without dealing with cultural factors), Raskin wrote an appendix called "The Biological Basis of Depression and Anxiety." This title itself reduces a complex dialectical development of coping, which she earlier described, to a "basis" that is biological.

She stated in this appendix: "Many familial diseases show this dual contribution of genes and environment: Diabetes, hypertension, heart disease, and cancer cluster in families but are not solely genetic" (p. 249). I do not argue with the idea that depression is partly biological, for surely everything in the mind is represented somehow in the brain. But once it is identified as a "disease" like those in this list, it becomes reified, with a noun for a name, and it becomes a topic in medical causality like cancer and diabetes. In a word, it becomes subject to a discourse, an intellectual treatment, that is blatantly reductive.

Watch the dialectic disappear as the discussion develops. First, the "specificity of familial predisposition to develop distinctive emotional illnesses is further evidence of the contribution of nature as opposed to nurture" (p. 249), which still allows the dual causality she expressed. Two pages later, in discussing polysomnographical findings, she noted the correlation between depression and particular electrical activity during sleep. Then she said, "Such results were among the early indications that depression has a biological basis, early evidence of the physiological disturbance in the disease of depression." The term *basis* here, which is frequent in such discussions, does not literally mean "cause." It could mean merely a physical correlate that is somehow "more basic," without specifying exactly how.

Two pages later, the reduction progresses: "Serotonin and norepinephrine stimulate activity in receptor cells. It makes intuitive sense that the absence of stimulating neurotransmitters would result in an emotional syndrome characterized by slowing: depression" (p. 254). This "result" is causal language, but it still holds open the (albeit narrowing) possibility of psychological factors in a dialectic of causality. The origin of this chain of causality could still be one's dealing with the world. But the completely reductive conclusion is also clearly stated in the same discussion: "If individuals with a particular illness show consistent abnormal activity levels in a certain anatomic region of the brain, it would be very difficult to view this as anything but evidence that the brain itself is the problem" (p. 252).

This may be simply an overstatement of the topic at hand, but it certainly displaces "the problem" from one's mental life to one's brain. The double bookkeeping with which Raskin started, and which she often analyzed with some care, is replaced by a reductive monism which is more than what Raskin called a "paradigm shift." It is good, old-fashioned, biological reductionism. It is a bias and a dogmatism all too common in Raskin's profession. That it appears in a sensitive and complex book like this one suggests the profound influence of culture—the culture of the profession of psychiatry, and the culture of American mastering of nature through science.

3. I have detailed much of this development in psychiatry in Keen (1998), Part I. For a vivid description of the current interpenetration of such theory, practice, and research, see Healy (1997).

4. Degan and Nasper (1996) offered a detailed analysis of this phenomenon. Part of the motivation of psychotics to avoid medicine is to avoid side-effects, but there is more to it. If one has been psychotic between the ages of 18 and 30, and then becomes symptom free at age 30, he or she will not have traversed the developmental tasks of establishing and refining an identity. Psychotherapy with such patients must not only work on that problem, made much more difficult because one's peers are mental patients, but it must also cope with mourning the loss of a decade of one's life.

chapter 5

DUALISM
AND
OBJECTIFICATION

In this and in chapter 6, I extend this argument from dualism to the problem that I eventually call *violence*. The connecting link is objectification.

Dualism, a philosophical theory, seems an unlikely candidate for the perpetration of violence. Of course, the theory itself is not violent. Dualism sets the scene and facilitates violence, but only under certain conditions—conditions that also seem rather innocent in the catalog of origins of violence. Dualism is a necessary but not sufficient condition for the violence described here.[1]

Dualism sets the scene for violence because we professionals are in denial that we assume it. By denying that humans are dualists, professionals first of all set ourselves up for theoretical simplicities that allow, or even encourage, such mammoth errors as lobotomy. If professionals had explicitly thought "the mind" to be something other than the brain, even though its fate is dependent on the brain, they would have avoided that blithe reductionism that allowed psychiatrists to experimentally disable the brains of thousands of people as was done at midcentury.

This problem still persists. "The mind" continues to be experienced as something separate from the brain, but the professional literature increasingly identifies mind with brain. Currently, professional opinion about "mind" seems to be something like "a function of" the brain, but also, more extremely, as a mere reifying name for the brain's "functioning." This view effectively cancels any respect, let alone reverence, for what might be amazement or wonder that there is human consciousness at all.

Rather than human consciousness as a brain function, we could see more than that. Consciousness is that by virtue of which we know about the brain, or about anything at all. It could be as sacred a ground as scientific mastery itself, which is wholly dependent on the miracle of consciousness. In the sixteenth century, the mind was akin to God, and we had reverence for it. We have removed this reverence for the mind not because we have placed it elsewhere; we seem to have lost it all together.

WHAT ARE WE TO DO WITH CONSCIOUSNESS?

To call human consciousness a miracle is not hyperbole. Consciousness is at the center of our humanity. Whatever one's relation to humanity, our relation to consciousness must be like it—but more intense. To the extent we respect, or are committed to, or have reverence for humanity, we ought to feel no less toward consciousness.

Consciousness is not something we understand; it is the prerequisite, rather, of all understanding. Such an interpretation, however, is not a part of the "culture of science."[2] To write about such a culture of science is difficult but necessary. Not knowing, and failing to criticize, that culture has consequences as dire as 40,000 or 50,000 lobotomies.

The culture of science denies humans are dualists, because science sees itself as having made philosophy obsolete. As a by-product of that victory, we are affirming some version of physical reductionism. Such an affirmation is a possible metaphysical position for a scientist to take, but it is a shaky platform from which to design the culture of our science, and thus humans' relationship to nature.[3]

That design sometimes includes little more than the goal of a mere mastery of nature. Human mastery of nature may have made sense when humans were not sure they could grow enough food. And when there are life-threatening diseases, they remain a part of nature that humans need to master. The culture of science assumes humans know what should be mastered and eliminated, but in the psychological professions, such a question becomes political, as multiple critics have pointed out (Leifer, 1969; Sarbin & Mancuso, 1980; Szasz, 1961). Worse still is any professional attempt merely to demonstrate control of consciousness "because it is there," thus a project of scientific pride.

We make consciousness into a thing in our reductionism; it becomes the object of our science. We are proud of our mastery, thus enacting the dualism we deny. It is a metaphysical jumble. In our lack of awareness of our metaphysical affirmations, and in the resulting design of the culture of science, we fail in that moment of critical reflection that should challenge us to distinguish our pride from our scientific calling.

Enacting Dualism

An analog for enacting dualism while denying it may be the way a strong person has contempt for a weak one. Such contempt does not feel like contempt to the strong one; one's superiority seems merely natural. But hidden in that superiority is a dependency. The strong need the weak in order for their strength to matter. Strength is nothing without the weak. Analogically, scientists are something more than they study; they are the origin and basis of all study. This superiority enacts dualism; it places scientists above what they study. But they do not dwell on that assumption. It simply feels natural, even as they see the objects of their study as "merely" objects. And even when the objects of study include the human mind itself.

In the culture of science, scientists do not see very clearly the options from which they choose how to understand themselves, but in their "normal science" mode, as scientists they are to themselves not objects but minds, subjects. There is philosophical baggage attached to that experience of self-as-scientist. A mind, the subject, does not occupy space nor time the way objects do.[4] It transcends objects. But its transcendence is dependent on objects just as strength is dependent on weakness.

There is, ironically for a culture of science, a curious parallel here to traditional cosmologies and theologies. Scientists relate to what they study as a god relates to its creation. They know it as an object that does not know them, just as a god knows humans but is not known by them. Both are relationships that are one-sided, and exactly nondialectical. Scientists do not see that the unconscious enactment of such a dualism is very similar to an unconscious enactment of being a god, a being who does or can know everything about the world, without examining self. Such a knower can only be worshipped. It is not an object and so it cannot be known. It is unknowable. Its nature is to know, not to be known.

Denying Dualism

I am arguing that all the aforementioned is determined by our philosophical tradition, which on the one hand operates according to a subject–object format, and on the other hand, denies it is a dualism. Everything science knows, then, must be an object that can be known and mastered. Scientists are proud of knowing the object world "out there," but in psychology particularly, they also know themselves by their objectifying themselves. Thus, scientists also claim to be a part of nature. That is their denial of dualism. To deny this denial is to say that scientists do not "objectify" the subject they are, as if they would reserve for themselves that space where only a god can be.

As scientists, we do both. We reduce ourselves to nature while our enactment rises above nature, and we stand above nature and deny that we do so.

This theoretical backdrop of science would be inconsequential except for the fact that the unconscious enactment of being a god leads us to an incredible and dangerous arrogance. One sign of this arrogance is the attitude with which we treat "sick minds." It should be said that we do not know what we are doing when, for example, we prescribe drugs to psychiatric patients. Of course, we do not know precisely what we are doing when we treat any illness. There is always more subtle knowledge that would make us better doctors. But we do, in medicine (unlike in witchcraft), have a working knowledge of human cells, tissues, and organs, and we can without shame tell our medical patients that we have a language that rationally describes the connections between our treatment and their suffering.

We do not know, in contrast, what we are doing in medicating psychiatric patients because the language in terms of which we envision brain, drugs, and diseases is a language that cannot tell us much at all about our clients' consciousness. It cannot reveal anything about fear, or guilt, or longing. There is no neurological description of meanings. It is ill-equipped to describe the interior of a human relationship. It bridges the gap from brain to such experiences with hunches and guesses and theories, all of which presume a kind of parallelism. Psychological "functions" have been named, but such naming reveals little of the hopelessness of the suffering patient before the doctor.

Practitioners "operate" on brains with drugs just as certainly as was done in lobotomy, although the medium is much less obviously invasive. Such operations manipulate the physical brain, perhaps yielding an improvement in the behavior and the consciousness of the patient. As such, we grasp the import of drugs in terms of the causal world of material things, including organisms. Thus, "electrotransmission among neurons, facilitated by neurotransmitters," is not a language that can tell us about the experiences or the meanings of human madness, or, for that matter, about sanity.

Although all this is true, the effect that is sought, in fact, is not in the brain; it is in the mind. We want the person who is deluded to recognize reality as we do; we want the obsessive to be able to control his or her own thoughts, the phobic his or her own fears, the depressive his or her own moods. Recognizing, having thoughts, fears, and most of all, controlling this symphony of mental life—all these are psychological, not physical, events. That they depend on the brain is obvious, but that they are not material events is equally obvious—which is why our dualism is obvious. If we could produce these results without intervening in the brain, we would gladly do so. The fact that we don't do that very efficiently (say, in conversational psychotherapy) leads us to operate on the brain as if the brain is the problem. Although brain defects and neurological diseases certainly are problems, it is plausible that the wildest delusional patient has a perfectly normal brain.

The fact that practitioners can affect experience by operating on the brain with instruments or drugs leads them to do it. They are changing the brain in such a way as to prevent what they do not want. Were they to give drugs to normal people, they would cure nothing because they would see no disease to cure. But they may be taking away from these people the ability to imagine wild and crazy things. Would practitioners prevent these people's art, or narrative creations, or religious ecstasy? There are no answers to such questions, but we steadfastly refuse to admit that any of these questions are relevant. Are we pretending, when actually we do not know what we are doing?

Since we do not take the mind seriously as central to the events of (their) mental illness, we may limit and destroy part of its (their) functioning along with changing their brain. Were we to take the mind seriously, we would approach it with much more care. By reducing the mind to the brain (in *their* case, at least), it becomes an "organ" of the body, like the kidney or heart, about which technological mastery is so impressive. But neither the kidney nor heart produces mind. They can be fixed or changed or even replaced without changing the center of the personal life of the person—the consciousness of the person.

RESISTANCE TO TECHNOLOGY

Divorcing the mind from the soul and seperating the soul from God were the historical movements that set up the tendency to see the mind as the brain and the brain as a machine that can be fixed. In the history of medicine, the causality of machines enlightened us about aspects of bodily functioning that scientists came eventually to master with impressive power. But these historical steps did not happen easily. Resistance to medical advances have often caused delay, even harm.

If the protests had been successful, they may have prevented scientific developments that led to the medical technology now depended on to cure the body. That resistance was undermined by scientific diligence, and, perhaps, also by a faith in technology from centuries of folk medicine that had experimented in the same way. As long as people have suffered, such bodily interventions have been invented. This activity has been going on for as long as there has been human culture.

Certainly part of the resistance to experimenting with medical technology in the early modern period came from the fact that the human body was experienced as an organ of the mind as fully as the mind is a function of the body. One's hands and fingers answer questions one's mind has about the world. One's eyes and ears do too, and they eventuate in the brain. Brain exudes mind, but in fact the whole body is mentalized. When one's leg is broken or one's finger is cut, the individual is there in the leg or finger; "I" am hurt. "I," the mental entity with an identity and a future, am there in the body. To invade it with instruments or chemicals is to invade the person. No wonder there was resistance.

In the history of medicine, resistance to a technology of the body was also based on religious and superstitious beliefs, implemented through political and legal means, and it resulted in persecutions and banishments. But the sense of the body as "me," and as "mine," as "mental" finally, as in some way too precious or even sacred to tamper with, was eventually overcome by medical successes and advances. Are we justified in expecting this same pattern in psychopharmacology? Or is such technology of the mind critically different?

As long as we deny our own dualism and allow ourselves the intellectual shortcut of treating the mind like a body, our confidence will lead us to expect such results. The body of *surgical* intervention was a minded body, but our theory was mechanistic and causal, stated in the language of physical events (or of medicine). The neglect of the mind portion of the minded body costs little; general anesthesia makes the minded body sleep. Mechanistic theory thus suffices. In contrast, *psychopharmacological* intervention aims at a *mental* change, which is a radical extension of the medical project that took care to not intervene in the mind. It too aims to intervene in something else, the functioning medical brain. However, that brain mediates the intervening in anything at all. At the very least, we should confess that we already presuppose some comprehension of a relation between the brain and ideas.

Because the details of intellectual accomplishment are beyond us, it behooves us to exercise caution. The present line of thought is not a blanket resistance to psychopharmacology, but it does advocate a moment of reflection. Intuitive resistance to psychopharmacology is in some ways like the earlier resistance to medical experimentation. It feels like an invasion of my body when I feel my body is "me." But unlike that case, my sense that my mind is "me" cannot be overcome by pretending that it is like the body, by pretending it is an object of physical medicine. The reflective pause provoked by psychopharmacology is more basic, and more urgent. We must be critical.

Psychopharmacology, as something to pursue, is a term that sounds like "electrochemistry," a field that explores the relation between phenomena of two formerly separate sciences. But the "psycho" in psychopharmacology refers to phenomena of a different order (*ordo cognoscendi*, not *ordo essendi*) and the term pretends to bridge two incommensurate languages and modes of understanding. But we do not know what we are doing. We fail to see this when we deny that we are dualists—or perhaps more precisely, when we deny that we operate simultaneously with two radically different orders of meaning. Such an intellectual failure lies beneath the debacles of lobotomy, is still operative in electroshock therapy, and in psychopharmacology. The intellectual failure, in the case of lobotomy, had vividly disastrous consequences.

In the case of psychopharmacology, the practical costs are more subtle than in lobotomy, and they are mixed with measurable successes, in psychological/mental terms. Yet we should not be surprised to be surprised later that the profession may have been unwittingly violent. This possibility should not be ignored, for as long as we reduce the mind to the brain, and assume the brain is an organ that can be fixed, we will try to fix it. And that can be violent. The lobotomy story is forgotten only at the peril of the profession and our patients.

THE COSTS OF MASTERING NATURE

The progress of science objectifies the world. Making the world an object denies it its subjectness. Subjectness, consciousness, is not an object of science, except as a function of the brain. As a function, it remains an object more than a subject. A function is not "me." I am no more reducible to a brain than I am to a machine. I am a person. But that category is missing from science—reduced to its parts and its functions.

The great divide between "me" and the natural object world makes the world different from me. I may be victimized by it, but I also master it. Human beings have a historical competition with it, and it (the natural world) is currently losing, except insofar as it will have its revenge on us all when the natural resources run out and we starve. But for the time being, nature is not of intrinsic value. It is to be used by Me and Us. Its value depends on our needs and wants. I am the subject and, as such, I am the center, that from which all else radiates. This is a consciousness of self and subjectness that objectifies the not-I, and robs it of its value. When we do this to persons, no less than nature, they are in danger of human rapacity.

Hence, there is a neglect of the subject (them), and an exaggeration of the subject (scientists) at the same time. What we don't have is a respectful grasping that we are subjectlike and objectlike, and so are our patients. This lack is a part of the culture of science that is dedicated to mastering nature. It risks having contempt for nature, and as it extends to the human sciences, it risks violence. Scientists proved they can master and defeat psychosis in lobotomy. The brain put up little resistance in the face of lobotomists, and those objectified subjects we called psychotics yielded to the violence. Our playing god and having contempt where we might have had reverence are obvious in this episode.

But lobotomy did not make psychotic patients yield to all our wishes. They did not yield to the desire to cure—a motive that comes from subjectifying (identifying with) others rather than objectifiying them, a motive that does not assume dualism, does not assume that some people are "mere nature" (disease) to which nothing is owed but mastery. Lobotomy satisfied science's objectifying desires—to defeat nature. It did not satisfy our humanistic desires, which lead to the medical desire to cure.

In the lobotomy struggle, scientists saw themselves divided within themselves. Insofar as they experienced patients as natural objects, patients were like an enemy to defeat, a threat to scientists' well-being. Scientists overcame them with force. It was easy to quiet the wards, as well as to quiet individual patients, but it was done violently. It is also fairly clear that such patients were not quite like the professionals; they were "psychotic," as we now say with medical detachment. But these same people, under different names, have only recently, and only in medically detached ways, graduated from being madmen and madwomen. Because the historic contempt for such people has outlasted the name change, the word *psychotic* has become tainted. And this traditional, older contempt has spread from the patients to the doctors, to the distribution of prestige in medicine, so that psychiatry is at the lowest rank among medical specialties.[5]

These are all facts of the scientific culture and the wider American or Western culture. This contempt is implicit in the motive to master mental illness by technological manipulation rather than by methods where conversation is used. Conversation is between equals; technological manipulation is between a scientist and his or her object. Conversation aims at understanding; technology aims at mastery. Scientific culture transported into the human sciences like psychiatry and psychology corrects its contempt in its obvious errors like lobotomy—although it was only after tens of thousands of such operations. And now, half a century later, scientific culture remains insensitive to more subtle manipulations.

Psychopharmacology is an example of such a subtle manipulation. Its easy legitimacy, the matter of fact attitude with which conversation and understanding are replaced with technology and mastery, shows that groundwork had been laid long before 1955 when Thorazine was introduced. The assumption of authority by medicine over the insane leads to the surrender of the reciprocities of moral treatment and to embracing the medicalization of madness. This medicalization is at least as old as Pinel and Benjamin Rush; it was the beginning of our technological attitude toward those called "mad."

MEDICALIZATION OF MADNESS

Medical concepts of disease certainly are justified in leading to a nullification of cancer, alien bodily processes that kill if they are not killed. But cancer survivors who have faced death closely often report that, although they are happy to have survived, they are also richer for the experience of the physical and spiritual struggle of facing the ultimate and inevitable shutdown of the physical body.[6] In the case of so-called "mental illness," the body object is not, as in the case of cancer, the scene of the struggle, but rather it is the spiritual subject that struggles. If one is psychotic, one struggles not with an object that is other, like a disease that must be nullified, but rather one struggles with struggling itself, overwhelmed by tragedy or terror or moral crisis or unanswered longing, a travail often derailed by fatigue and desperation.

What appears alien seems to be seen as worthy of elimination, as in "disease." But a delusion, hallucination, obsession, or unspeakable fear, is not alien. It is one's struggle with life itself, usually incomprehensible to others, and often even to oneself. The repeatedly unsuccessful effort to face the tragedy, endure the terror, satisfy the longing, or answer the moral crisis—and sometimes all these at once—is uncanny in its frustration. What is contended in mental illness is not alien; it is not other; it is the person caught up, fascinated with or horrified by him or herself struggling unproductively, repetitively, exhaustingly, with none other than life.

Could our violence toward schizophrenic persons reflect the fact that we become *intolerant* of and try to nullify struggles we do not understand? We want it to be over; we want it to disappear. But the more we convince ourselves that such experiences should be nullified, made into nothing, the more we surrender the conversation, and the more we close ourselves off from what such people have to teach us. The more we teach those we call schizophrenic to nullify their own struggle, the more we undermine *their* engaging it. And the more we, as a "scientific culture," forgo the safeguards of conversation, the more we become dangerous in our techniques of mastering psychosis, techniques that negate its struggle and its meaning.

There seems little doubt that what is called "schizophrenia" consists of feelings and thoughts that can be unproductive as well as incomprehensible to others and to ourselves; it can be repetitive, exhausting, and spiritually draining. There seems little doubt also that this activity can be discouraged, or relieved considerably, by lobotomy, by electroshock, or by antipsychotic drugs. Patients are persuaded or coerced both to see their struggle as alien and as illness, and to undergo these nullifications. We want them to relieve themselves of these struggles, and we want to relieve ourselves of having to deal with people engaging in such struggles as well. But in relieving ourselves of the burden of them, we are engaging in the project of mastering nature, directed at someone else whom we call now "other." When we ask or advise patients to so relieve themselves of the burden of themselves through such technologies, we are asking them to call part of themselves "other" as well. In coming chapters, the extent to which this objectification has gone is discussed.

Insofar as this mastery project nullifies the mental life of a schizophrenic by cataloging it as *disease*, to that extent we professionals are engaging in a kind of institutional violence. This topic is taken up in chapter 7, but first (in chapter 6), I examine objectification, at its philosophical, theoretical, and practical levels.

NOTES

1. Violence in real life is not simple. Subtle forms, as perpetrated against most mental patients, are a joint product of personal angers, professional traditions, and a society's climate of legitimate violence. Some of the following are rarely called *violence* even though they are correlated with events that are violent, such as the correlation between lobotomy and Nazism, and between domestic battering and the Vietnam War. See for example Bell (1985) on prisons, Blackstock (1975) on government persecutions, Cleaver (1994) on the bombing of MOVE, Dobash and Dobash (1979) on domestic violence, Hutchings (1952) on family violence, Marshall (1991) on "drug wars," Matthiessen (1989) on violence toward the American Indian Movement, Reiman (1988) on social class violence, Schecter (1982) on battery of women, and Wright and Sheley (1991) on urban teenagers.

The ways people hurt one another, and the ways we manage to call it something other than violence, are legion. Was it violent for American Savings and Loans to squander the life savings of thousands of elderly people, who thus were forced to spend their last years in abject poverty? In police terms, theft differs from assault, but think of the experience of the victims. Elias points out, in addition, that official reaction to such events is often understood to be adequate by the population only if "the crime" is defined as solvable by violence (i.e., punishing the perpetrators). Such official violence, then, like how mental patients are treated, sets the stage for personal violence through a climate of legitimate violence.

This crime–punishment (personal–professional) cycle of violence is widespread and is an unfortunate, often invisible, but undeniable part of the tradition of hospital psychiatry. Smith (1997) described in detail how the narratives of civil society are central in legitimating violence of all kinds in modern society.

2. This sentence suggests a contrast that is developed in the next section, between an analytic approach, which characterizes the scientific tradition, and a dialectic approach, which characterizes politics. The *analytic* project of science is manifested in technology, where the lived space of the activity surrounds the subject–scientist in the center, and the surrounding world becomes his object. A *dialectic* space, in contrast, is two-sided, each party facing different parts of the world, as well as facing one another.

A dialectic project creates a space like that of Plato's dialogues. The existence of at least two perspectives on the same issue in a dialectic process limits the outcome to what the two subjects can see, each from his own point of view and from what each takes to be the other's. It does not guarantee truth, for the two parties may share a bias and agree to indulge it.

The analysis of the world, including psychiatric illnesses, negates a real conversation and invites successive analytic distinctions that seek a "basic unit" or underlying ground, of which modern medical theory is made: microorganisms, the cell, neurotransmitters, and so on. A dialectic approach, although it fails to promise the certainty that comes with uncovering a more basic level of analysis, parlays the difference in perspective into always further explorations of different starting points.

3. There is a very particular duplicity in our implicit assumptions about science. On the one hand, we are aware that our perception involves a particular angle of vision, the notation for which is coded in our knowledge in the form of operational definitions. On the other hand, knowledge itself has no location in physical space. It is also possible to understand knowing as having no location in the usual sense at all. We might say that a person knows, and that person, or her brain, is in a Newtonian location, but of course much knowing is shared. It is in many minds at once, and in books, and in the structure of social institutions, and so on. Knowing "resides in" a culture, which really, like mind itself, has no location in physical space.

4. Given this implicit self-exaltation by the scientific mind, the low status of psychiatry is ironic. Our cultural contempt for mental patients is made worse by our cultural pride in the mental mastery of the world by science. Furthermore, managed care has added another blow to psychiatry's stand-

ing. One indication of the loss of prestige of psychiatry within medicine in general is its unattractiveness to medical students, indexed, for example, by the drop of nearly 12%—to 3,909 from 4,447—between 1988 and 1994, of U.S. medical school graduates in psychiatric residencies. Gabbard (1992) referred to this effect as "the big chill."

5. See note 4 for some details about the low status of psychiatry.

6. A recent effort to describe this phenomenon was made by Broyard (1992).

chapter 6

OBJECTIFICATION AND VIOLENCE

Objectification is the word I use to describe seeing something as an object. When individuals see things as objects, they separate them from themselves, create a distance, and adopt an attitude toward them that is capable of either attachment or detachment. People are attached to many of the objects in their daily lives; they like their cars, their desks, their clothes, and shoes and hats. They do not want to sell any of these things, but if they were to put prices on these things (as happens at auctions), they would see them through the eyes of others, judge what they are "worth" to others, thus bypassing the attachment they have toward them and taking up an attitude of detachment toward them.[1]

In such an attitude it is said that people are more "objective," by which is meant exactly a bypassing of one's personal attachment and a judging of things impersonally, in the name of no one in particular, or in the name of others whose values are known but not shared. Such an attitude is sometimes necessary for success, in settings ranging from judging a market if one is a producer of goods, to athletic competitions and other social contexts. And this attitude is crucial to science, for science is a body of knowledge that bears the signature of no particular perceiver but rather states the dimensions of things seen in their own terms. Leaving aside the complexity of postmodern critiques for the time being, we can say that science is the ultimate in impersonal perception.

A particular kind of attitude thus emerges when speaking of objective knowledge of persons, as social and psychological sciences must do. That attitude is one of impersonal knowledge of persons. That means, in its best sense, that they can be seen, described, and studied in themselves rather than according to prior attachments or agendas that would blind one to some things and accentuate others. To bypass that attachment or agenda is what social and psychological scientists try to do when they "do" science. But that impersonal knowledge does not necessarily *depersonalize* the people studied. They do not have to be made into literal *things* for scientists to be objective about them. All that is needed is that distance that rules out particular biases grounded in something personal in oneself as observer.

However, surgeons may well go beyond this degree of objectification, for their skills are so precise that the appendix they ablate becomes totally a technical object, an object of their technique and technology. It no long remains human at all. Surgery is not a personal transaction; it is impersonal and, beyond that, it depersonalizes. One appendectomy had better be like another, without variation shaped by attachments, or even by humanizing the patient. It is wise, therefore, for this procedure to be about techniques and outcomes and not about people at all. I forgive my surgeon for forgetting it is me on the table because I do not want him to do it for me; I want him to do it because it is his job, and I want his commitment to be to his technical expertise, not to our relationship. And I want to be anonymous.

Is this a model for how to do psychiatry and psychology? There are ways in which the answer must be "yes," and there are ways in which it must be "no." Patients want no bias in their treatment; they want to be seen objectively. They want to be objectified, but there is a limit. For they are not things, and at some point seeing them as objects has gone too far.[2] To gauge that point is not easy, but it surely can be said that when lobotomists did what they did to persons' brains and minds, they had gone too far. Their technology had become so depersonalized that they did not see clearly what they were doing. What can be said about psychopharmacology on this dimension? Do psychopharmacologists go too far?

I argue here that often they do, and that when they do it, they do it because of the enactment of dualism, concomitant with its denial. They do it because they cleanse their relationship not only of their own involvement with the patient, but also because they cleanse their concept of the patient of that warmth of humanity on which the patient depends. Patients depend on surgeons to give that warmth up; and they depend on psychiatrists not to. Surgeons do a kind of violence, and patients expect them to do it well; psychiatrists can also depersonalize their patients, but patients dare not let them do it in good conscience.[3]

In terms of the previous chapter, it may be said this way. Insofar as practicing psychopharmacology is dualistic in the enactment of superiority to the subject matter, that subject matter is viewed as mere brain matter. Thus, persons are depersonalized and the approach to violence begins. Insofar as we deny our dualism and pretend that we are not pretending when we say we rise above the mind–brain with the objectifications of dualism, we compound the error and are likely to perform violently. In this chapter, we must say it less abstractly.

PSYCHOPHARMACOLOGICAL THEORY

It is not really established, but it is a coherent theory that serotonin activity in the brain is lessened somehow with depression, and that drugs that inhibit the re-uptake of serotonin from the synaptic cleft enhance that activity, which in turn relieves the depression. When one says this of oneself, one can cheerfully pop a Prozac[4] and expect to feel better, and the act is no more violent than having a snort of whiskey. But insofar as practitioners teach their patients to do as they do, they are bringing to bear the legitimacy of science on a process that objectifies the mentalized body, that transforms the mind–brain into the objectified and impersonalized brain. The site of the problem to the psychopharmacologist is the brain in the same way that the site of Streptococcus lanceolatus in the lung causes pneumonia. The problem becomes internal, a brain problem. Mind objectified into brain reduces it to the level of the lung. The lung, too, may be necessary for consciousness, but not in the way that the brain is. This objectification depersonalizes the individual.

People get depressed because of their lives, and their brain may change as a result of that.[5] And this change may make it difficult to change their lives. But if they are told that taking the pill cures their disease called depression, it is an extension of objectification from a minded brain to a mere organ. This, too, depersonalizes. It not only objectifies their mental grasp of the object world, transforming consciousness into an object, it often negates the patient's obligation to deal with the world differently. And it reduces the complexity of life to a simplicity few neuroscientists would accept. In addition to all these errors, it falsifies to the client both the nature of the relationship they have to the doctor and to the world, and it falsifies the nature of the depression they presumably "have."

Depression can be called a disease, of course, but that objectification already depersonalizes considerably. To say that one's inability to conclude a period of mourning a death in the family is Major Depressive Disorder is to say that the person's condition is essentially like that of other patients classified in that category, even though they have not necessarily experienced a death in the family, and they certainly have not had the very personal relationship the mourning patient had to the lost family member. The similarity is in terms of mere *symptoms*, like sleeplessness, lack of appetite, inability to concentrate, prolonged sadness, and preoccupation with death. It has nothing to do with the person who was lost and the changes the patient must make in his or her life in order to cope with that loss sufficiently to rejoin the currently neglected remainder of his or her life. If there is a similarity, it is impersonal indeed.

Furthermore, what this patient is going through may indeed seem protracted to others, or even to the patient, and neither they nor the patient may recognize why this loss is so difficult to deal with. But classifying the patient's experience as a mental illness adds nothing to that understanding. What in fact is needed is an exploration of the patient's life, the place of that relationship in it, how it echoes historical facts and meanings, how the patient's angers and fears and guilts made the deceased person central to the patient's sense of self, and so on. If a pill helps the patient, it does not help with these explorations, although it might make them a bit easier to undergo. What is abundantly clear is that no pill can substitute for the mental work the patient must do.

Although this example is relatively simple, what is called *depression* is often complicated by the fact that the "losses" to which one must adjust may not have been experienced as losses at all.[6] What was central to the individual's sense of self may have changed without announcing itself as clearly as does a death in the family. And yet the same exploration is necessary. Even in cases of clearly documented "recurrent episodes" of depression, where it is especially tempting to see these experiences as "disease," and hence as biological in origin and in treatment, no biological "correction" operates by itself.

In addition to an information-processing machine or an evolutionarily shaped organism, I am a person who remembers and anticipates my own life. These mental activities are affected by this "disease," and they may be activities that effect it—if one's thoughts are called a disease. With respect to such thoughts, the work one must do cannot be understood in terms of the chemistry of the brain. It can only be understood in terms of meanings in one's life.

The displacement of "depression" from meanings in one's life to chemicals in one's brain is illicit in exactly that depersonalizing way that lobotomy theory displaced the "mental illness" of tens of thousands of patients from meanings in their lives to a disease in their brain. The violent surgery of lobotomy was premised on a very thin theoretical connection between the frontal lobes and the limbic system in the brain—a connection that lobotomy was intended to disrupt. Indeed, the "person," as we usually understand a person, does not appear in this theory.[7]

What exactly is left out of account was the fact that the consciousness of the individual is not an organ, or even merely a function, in the usual sense. Consciousness is, within the human sphere, the closest thing we have to a genuine mystery. We cannot explain how I am conscious. It is a phenomenon we understand no better than the meaning of life itself. If ever there ought to be an attitude approaching reverence in psychiatry, it is here, connected to recognizing how unlike a scientific object consciousness is, and how likely we are, in treating it as one, to be violent.

Of course, lobotomy is certainly more vividly destructive than what is done to the brain with pills. In fact, it is possible (but not established) that many pills have no adverse effects on the brain at all. But any comfort lent by that thought is immediately compromised by the realization, born of re-personalizing the patient, that they too have important work to do in their lives—their relationships, their values, goals, concepts, and feelings toward the world, both currently and in the past.

To treat depression with antidepressant medication, without careful attention to the person's life, is to depersonalize the person. Often psychopharmacological treatment is accompanied with no such attention.[8] The violence here is not perpetrated against the brain of such persons (although that rarely can be ruled out completely), it is perpetrated against consciousness, against this person's consciousness, which is to say, against the person's life.

In its least case, this violence[9] is a violence of neglect, to which is often added the practitioner's confident reassurances that such neglect is harmless, and that such changes in one's life that might alleviate one's suffering need not be tended to.

Neglect is not simply passive aggression. People of all kinds do suffer, and to fail to address the person suffering is hardly unique to psychopharmacology. This neglect, however, reminds me of the neglect that is traditional in our and in many cultures' approach to such suffering that is hard to understand. I walk into the state hospital near my home and I find people whose families have rejected them, whose wives and husbands pretend they do not exist, whose former friends do not remember them, whose children are ashamed of them. This is neglect, but it is motivated by the meaner stuff of judgmental dismissal from the rolls of humanity. Medical neglect is more likely accidental, but that does not make it more excusable.

METAPHORS IN PSYCHIATRIC PRACTICE

An important feature of the medical neglect in psychiatry has to do with the professionwide trend in the use of language. It is no secret that the advances in neuropsychology and psychopharmacology are impressive, and that they are leading more and more to biological reductionism, which creates more objectification and more violence. The culture of science as it appears in psychiatry leads to an increasing tendency to use biological language, even when it is not appropriate. Biological metaphors like struggling to "digest" or "assimilate" an experience can be quite vivid and even helpful, for there is a metaphoric homology between, say, surviving a trauma and "metabolizing" a poison.

Problems appear, however, when practitioners begin to confuse the metaphoric use of terms with the literal use of terms. As metaphors become more biological, there is a tendency to take them literally even when their literal meaning constitutes a bias or an error. When doctors say that there is "a chemical imbalance in the brain," they are speaking not literally but metaphorically. The content says that something that should balance something else is not doing so, which creates an image of the dynamics of hormone regulation, for example, which controls one's sexual excitement or tendency to fight or flee.

The doctor's shift from literal to metaphoric communication is not an obvious one, because so much of communication is metaphorical. However, in science, where language is operationally defined, every word refers to a single meaning, and every one with the precision of quantification. Metaphor, in contrast, is possible because of the multimeaninged, layered character of natural language. Doctors who say this are not only speaking metaphorically, they have also chosen for their metaphor a quantitative concept ("balance") that further conceals the fact that the literal meaning of what is being said has no correspondence in our knowledge. Hence, it is doubly misleading.

Of course, because most language is "natural" instead of "scientific," most language is imprecise in its meaning and full of connotations. All psychotherapy, for example, is metaphoric. If a psychiatrist says to a client that "your father really was too busy to tend your needs," it is not simply a literal statement, for the phrase "your needs" refers to many things already addressed in the therapy, as will also be true of "too busy." Thus, it is a multilayered communication that is just as imprecise as saying "you were an orphan" or "you have a chemical imbalance in your brain."

The difference between the psychotherapeutic case and the medical one, however, is that in the latter the doctor is speaking within a scientific context, a context whose metaphors generally do not pretend a precision that is not there. If a cardiologist says that a patient's "heart sounds like a broken pump," it is not misleading in implying that this is information that medical science has mastered.

In fact, cardiology is well developed. The "pump" is well understood, as are its various ways of being broken. In the case of the supposed "chemical imbalance," on the other hand, medical science does not in fact know what chemicals are involved (although some of them may be known), nor where in the brain it matters (although we may know one place or two, tentatively), nor what will happen to this or thousands of other chemical balances in the brain if a psychotropic drug is put into the blood stream.

In other words, the phrase is an unconscious metaphor, with little care given to what it actually says, either literally or metaphorically. It is used only pragmatically, as a phrase that helps portray the doctor's calm confidence and to palliate a patient the doctor does not understand. Such an occurrence qualifies as "neglect" insofar as it directs the patient's attention away from relevant life issues that are depressing him or her. Unfortunately, it also leads to psychopharmacological prescription, whose consequences in the brain are understood imperfectly, and whose consequences in the life of the patient depends very much on what exactly the patient is experiencing, when and why. When these are insufficiently taken into account, it is clear that the neglect can be a serious invasion of the patient's conscious-ness with little regard for the violations of the integrity of the patient's life goals. Neglect becomes violence.

NONVIOLENT HELP

Good treatment is not always "nonviolent." Surgery is violent; it violates boundaries of body and self in multiple ways, and psy-chopharmacology may be violent to one's life, but it needn't be. Like surgery, it may be a risk worth taking when there is appropriate attention to one's larger life conflicts and struggles as well. To oper-ate surgically in emergencies, when there will be no one to help the patient understand what has been done to his or her body, may still be a risk worth taking. The body's capability to heal itself is well understood, and doctors give it a chance to do just that, hoping to have changed the odds in favor of the suffering person.

The other risk in psychiatry, of treating someone without medi-cine, will more likely be nonviolent. But it may also be less fast-act-ing, or even less effective in the shorter run. Nonviolence may not, therefore, always be the treatment of choice. But we can at least be assured that it will presuppose the respect granted to persons. It will eschew the reduction of a life to a brain. And most of all it will respect the "symptoms" as aspects of one's trying to cope with one's life rather than calling them signs of a "disease."

Diseases are scientific objects against which professions have been dedicated to eliminate them. Diseases are not respected in the sense of saying that they have a right to exist. The medical profession has committed itself, professionally, socially, and historically, to wiping them out. Thus, technology is appropriate to the task. One needn't respect the rights of a disease, one simply does battle and defeats it. There is no point in taking seriously the disease's point of view.

In contrast, psychiatry deals with men, women, and children who are experiencing crises in their lives. The first obligation of the psy-chiatrist is to listen, and the second is to speak. Thus, the method of nonviolent help that is most common is conversation. A conversation is clearly between two persons. In a conversation, Person A has to listen to what Person B says in order to offer what he or she has to say in response, or it is not a conversation but a set of directives. The action is between two minded bodies, or in shorthand, between two minds. It is not the doctor's mind exploring the patient's brain, the way the doctor looks at a diseased liver or listens to an arrhythmic heart. It is an exchange between fully personalized and embodied persons.

WHEN IS PSYCHOPHARMACOLOGY NOT HELPFUL?

If conflict is viewed as a part of life, and pain is considered a part of conflict, then medicating pain may well be unhelpful, or even harmful.[10] *Conflict*, as used here, refers to a conflict between oneself and important others in one's life, or it might mean an internal conflict such as a simultaneous desire and fear about the same course of action. *Pain* means either the anxiety, the depression, or the ennui that follows from struggling to resolve what seems an unresolvable situation. Sometimes such struggles are, of course, years long, or even lifelong. Some of us are born into them.

If the pills turn out to relieve the pain of the conflict, it may follow that the patient is better able to handle the conflict, for the depression may have been sapping the patient's energy or spoiling his or her relationships. There is no question that medication sometimes works exactly like this. But it is also possible that the pain of that conflict was an important ingredient in the patient's dealing with it. If, for example, the pain was anxiety that motivates the patient to start a new project, or change something importantly askew in his or her life, then elimination of the pain would interfere with the patient making the correction he or she really needs to make. To neglect such conflicts that are painful is sometimes best, but often the anxiety or the depression is an important part of one's experience, a part that makes it possible for the patient to interpret the experience well.

Either way, if relief of the pain either helps me to deal with or to neglect the conflict, I will have become a somewhat different person by muting the anxiety or depression I felt without the medication. However, that difference has more consequences than merely how I deal with the conflict. Those people in the immediate social context within which I move and live will adjust to any such difference in myself, and I will respond to their adjustment with an adjustment of my own. This dialectic between me and my friends and relatives will exaggerate the initial impact of the medicine, an impact that we have seen could be either helpful or harmful. It is also important to see that this indirect but nonetheless real change is a drug effect that is virtually impossible to predict, as dialectical processes so often are.

A dialectical process over time is like a conversation. I say X, to which you reply with Y, to which I reply with Q, to which you reply with R. Conversations often wander away from the original agenda of either party; in fact, the only conversations that do not do so must be intentionally controlled, consciously and concertedly, by one of the conversers, which is experienced by the other one as not being taken seriously. Human development itself has such an unpredictability, where a small difference in how a parent treats identical twins may lead them in increasingly divergent directions, even to distinct and markedly different personalities.

If my initial reaction to taking the drug is an improvement, then those in my immediate social context may welcome the change in me and all will go well. Of course, my handling something better because of a drug may also be an unwelcome surprise to someone who has a stake in my being the way I was before I took the drug. My getting "better" because of the drug may lead them into "worse" directions that no one would have predicted. By the same token, if the drug leads me not to improvement but to neglect a lesson-teaching conflict, this too might feed into the dialectic with others in either a helpful or harmful way. For example, it is possible that my neglect will motivate others to do more for me, and that enables me to do more for them, enhancing the closeness and gratification of the relationship for us all. But equally possible is a deterioration of the relationship as a result of my change.

Relationships often exist in highly structured networks of relationships—like a family, or a group of close friends. The face-to-face system itself is embedded in a number of larger systems that are less personal but no less dialectical. If my relationships with colleagues improve, it might provoke competing groups of colleagues to compete harder, or cheat in the competition—numerous possibilities so unpredictable as to constitute that uncertainty already known as real life. To follow through the ripples of change after the initial change brought on by a chemical discloses all the imponderable elements of influence in "how things turned out," among which the taking of a drug to relieve some pain may seem a small matter.

What becomes troublesome, if not outrageous to common sense, in the common practice of psychopharmacology today is that little or none of this is taken into account. To do so requires that the prescriber follow the patient's life in some detail, as in psychotherapy, in order to make the most of good effects or minimize the bad ones. When psychotherapy is the context of pharmacotherapy, there remains a "human element" in the treatment—by which I mean, of course, a "mental" guide and not merely a highly abstract, speculative, and radically incomplete neurochemical theory about how a little more serotonergic activity would be a good thing.[11]

Much current theory and practice involve professional neglecting of the life of the person for whom medication is prescribed. We are obliged to call it a violation of boundaries, perhaps ethical, perhaps a violence of unrequited trust. But, however that judgment is settled, what is not escapable is that taking pills has changed the patient. His or her consciousness of the original conflict has been transformed, his or her understanding of self and life has become more hidden. Eliminating the pain has concealed from the patient something that may, indeed, have made things much worse, but eliminating it may also have concealed an edge of consciousness without which the patient is a less acute observer. And with the successive dialectical elaborations, such a change becomes permanent.

SOME IMPLICATIONS

I have argued that conversation, as opposed to medication, is likely to be less violent than medication. Of course, not all conversations are nonviolent. One may impose and hurt and ridicule another with mere words. But nonviolent conversation can be accomplished with good will and respect. Beyond that, one wants expertise from a therapist, but that too, although at its best it maybe"objective," or even perhaps "scientific" in the way just described, is not necessarily violent. Expertise need not depersonalize the way surgery or psychopharmacology does, not even in the more subtle way that diagnosis does.

Most of all, the "respect" of nonviolent helping implies that the individual is doing as well as he or she can, and that the efforts, no matter how symptomatic and self-defeating, are efforts to deal with certain situations or problems. These efforts may have to change, but they are valuable. They address something in one's life that has to be attended to. They are oneself; they are one's attempt to live, to have something or be somehow or be someone.

People ask for help when they are in situations with which they have to struggle, and when the struggle is not going well. Sometimes they are born into this struggle, sometimes it is less inevitable, sometimes it needs to be redefined, or brought into awareness, or worked on more concertedly. Such people are suffering not from diseases but from the travails and troubles of life. Beyond that, a person asks for help surrounding issues of her or his personal life narrative, the conclusion of which, the point of which, lies ahead in some as yet indeterminate way. The most central question of such issues is some version of the question, "Who am I to be?"

It is the obligation of the practitioner to deal centrally with this question because this is the question with which the patient is most centrally dealing. Patients may not want to ask such questions, for they find the direction of their lives in general to be just fine. "It is just that I have this little problem. . . ." Sometimes a therapist must let this self-presentation stand, but there are certainly other times when "this little problem" betrays something beyond itself. That something is embedded in a relationship, or a job, or a family arrangement that in fact is not livable without exacting the cost of the symptoms. When a practitioner cures the symptoms without reference to the problem, is done violence to the person. It is to suppose that one knows that "depression" (as if that were one thing, a disease) is "caused by a chemical imbalance in the brain."

We practitioners do not know that. We lie when we say that. It is a simplification designed to bypass the complications of psychotherapy. A practitioner may have her or his reasons to do just that, reasons that have to do with the availability of funds to pay for treatment, or the schedule imposed by the bureaucracy that manages the funds, and so on. But this pretended expertise exacts a cost too great, a neglect of the conflicts in one's life, the options and feelings and memories, and of course the consciousness that frames it all, and the narrative that organizes it all.

To neglect these things is to neglect the person. To neglect the person is to violate the person, to play fast and loose with the integrity of what the person is trying to do. The professional superstructure of diagnostic language, scientific traditions, bureaucratic supports—all of these pillars of professional expertise may be undermining the treatment, and it is the singular treatment professional who is caught in the dilemma of either doing what is best for the person facing her or him, or doing what all these supporting structures dictate. It is not an easy time to be a psychiatrist, or a clinical psychologist, or a psychiatric nurse, or a psychiatric social worker.[12]

This discussion must move, then, from violence considered here as an abstract category all practitioners get caught up in, where "the practitioner" has been a detached individual, making professional decisions, to the question of institutional violence, violence generated not by practitioners but by institutions. The paradigm case presented in the next chapter is one that exaggerates the foibles of the diagnostic system into treatment that commits "violence" in the sense described abstractly in this chapter.

NOTES

1. The term *objectification* is common among phenomenological psychologists. Grounded in a subject–object format, which itself reflects (but is not identical to) Cartesian dualism, objectification is something like "reification," although the distinction between objectifying something legitimately and doing so illegitimately is often very subtle. In the text, I focus on how objectification goes with detachment. Another accompanying aspect of this experience is consolidating processes or events into stable, thing-like entities or properties. Fischer (1978) offered a particularly telling example of the subtlety of this second objectification:

Thus, Daniel's teacher says, "I keep thinking that he had more potential, but when he doesn't score well on the achievement tests, I think maybe he's just not intelligent enough after all," and at first this teacher is unable to say just what he had experienced as Daniel's "potential."

Fischer continued by pointing out the following.

Eventually, as I encourage focusing on actual events, the teacher shakes off earlier conceptions and discovers more alive recollections of Daniel leaning forward in his seat during lectures, asking questions in an excited manner, and requesting extra resources for a class project.

She concluded, "Later, as he watches Daniel in class, he sees with a vision that is attentive to process and context. He now sees differently" (p. 219).

Maintaining a personal attachment to an object invests it with my self and compromises the "objectivity" of the "thing-in-itself" in my perception. Fischer's example shows that the objectification falsified Daniel's activity and behavior into a trait. This "objectification" falsifies rather than purifies. Scientific objectification tries to increase detachment and overcome attachment in the faith that such detachment purifies perception and increases veridicality of perception. But Fischer's example shows how it can also reify and falsify perception. In the present context, objectification is assumed by science to be good, whereas the argument of the chapter argues that it can be quite mixed, even harmful to perception.

2. Some psychopharmacological literature is quite explicit about avoiding this excess. See, for example, Preston et al. (1997, foreword).

3. Romanyshyn (1989), without demonizing technology, viewed a danger in our lack of reflection about its increasing influence—not so much in its mere power, as in the atomic bomb, but in its effect of exaggerating our tendency to distance ourselves from our humanity.

The bomb is *not* an exterior thing lying outside the circumstances of our living. If it is the final act it is not the period of the last sentence in the story of technology. Rather, it is already written into the letters and words, the sentences and the paragraphs, which make up the tale. (p. 22)

His conclusion is arresting: "In the everyday acts of distancing, the bomb has already been armed. Indeed, in a sense, it has already exploded" (p. 22).

In itself, objectification, as a kind of distancing, can be helpful when it is a temporary look from another angle of vision. But the identification of one's sadness as a disease without a full appreciation of what one is sad about, what one may able to do about it, how it forces one to change one's life, and so on, leads to an application of chemistry to the experience whose power may be more destructive than is thought.

4. Prozac is believed to act exactly this way on serotonin and thus is called a selective serotonin re-uptake inhibitor, or SSRI.

5. The correlations between brain events and mental events have been often verified. Furthermore, it is likely that the causality goes both ways. For the long-term effect of repeated mental events on the brain, see Baxter et al. (1992).

6. This has been understood, although neglected, since Freud (1917/1959).

7. For a look at the mid-century literature, see Fulton (1951). I develop this point at length in Keen (1998) *Drugs, Therapy, and Professional Power: Problems and Pills.*

8. It is appropriate at this point to recall that more than 75 percent of psychotropic drugs like antidepressants are prescribed by primary care physicians, that is, general practitioners. Less than 25 percent are prescribed by psychiatrists, and of those, not all are dealt with personally, within a "personal" relationship containing features that deserve this adjective.

9. The use of the term *violence* in connection with these matters is not hyperbole. *Violence* is related to *violate*, which means to ravish, profane, desecrate, among other things. When we do this, we disregard a sense of some-

thing's integrity, which we ought to respect, or something's status as commanding our reverence, or something's sanctity, or sacredness. In the secular humanistic West, we still hold persons sacred; we still have an obligation of reverence in the face of the beginning or the end of a human life. And if anything is sacred to us, it is our right and ability to flourish. Violations of any of this are violent. Certainly, the connotative stakes go up when we deal with things sacred, but there is violence in neglect, by parents or by doctors. Elias (1997) referred to ours as a "culture of violent solutions" and he also explained elsewhere (Elias, 1993) how language is used to perpetrate violence. On reflection, it appears that the inability to see one's own violence is increasing in proportion to the growing inability to experience reverence or to identify anything as "sacred."

10. There are certainly those who argue that drugging ourselves or each other as a way to cope with anguish is never justified. Breggin (1991, 1994) is very close to that position, as is Illich (1976). There is no need here to go that far, for the mindless overprescription of psychotropic medicines offers us much to criticize. Psychiatrists themselves have a tradition of skepticism about psychopharmacology, beginning with the memory that Thorazine was sometimes resisted in the 1950s, and Tofranil, the antidepressant, in the 1960s (Healy, 1997; Wortis, 1965), and augmented by periodic outcries about overprescription (e.g., Greenblatt & Shader, 1971).

11. I have developed this point in chapter 7 of Keen (1998); the chapter is called "Is the Psychology of Pharmacotherapy the Active Ingredient?"

12. I call attention here to the discussion in footnote 1 of chapter 4.

INSTITUTIONAL VIOLENCE IN PSYCHIATRY AND PSYCHOLOGY

The violence of lobotomy was personal. One person inserted an ice picklike object above the eyeball into the eye socket of another person, with the tap of a small hammer penetrated the cranium, then swooshed the instrument back and forth, severing millions of brain connections. It was an act of violence, but it differs from the violence of crime on the streets, or violence in the houses of abusive husbands, wives, and parents. Lobotomy was not only personal, it was quite impersonal. Practitioners did not know their clients well. They held no ill will toward them, and they realized little immediate profit because of their practice.

What is so remarkable about lobotomy was the institutional support for it. It was a sociological and political phenomenon as surely as it was personal and professional. In fact, its popularity has led to an appreciation of how institutions perpetrate violence, even as they seem to be offering good will, such as medical treatment. A part of institutional violence is that the perpetrators are supported; they do not need to hide what they are doing from the authorities in the institutional context. The person who lobotomized another in 1950 was enacting a script he or she may have had little personal stake in. This is the signature of institutional violence.

We are familiar with concentration camps, and other results and by-products of war. In this enormously violent century, we have come to accept institutional violence, for it has become so integral a part of modern cultures that it hardly feels like violence at all. Even the Nazi commandant who gave the order for executions at a rate of hundreds at a time was convinced that although his job was unpleasant, it was not violent.[1] Nazism is over, but much of the cultural support of violence is not. It is important to see clearly what a culture looks like when it mistakes its own violence for necessity, or even for medical treatment or loving kindness.

Here, I look first, at an intermediate case of institutional violence, which accompanied (especially) trade relations with the Orient in the seventeenth to the twentieth centuries.. The violence was begun before the bombs of World War II began falling. It was done in our heads, in our fearful protection of ourselves and our empires and our wealth. Hussein Abdilahi Bulhan (1985) stated: "From the fourteenth century to the present, Europe and its descendants have been embarked on an unprecedented mission of violence and self-aggrandizement throughout the world" (p. 37). Such an extreme claim becomes believable the more one looks. And so I must begin here with a look at our culture in order to understand how humans operate, even in the "treatment professions," and what we would do were we to try to be less violent.[2]

ORIENTALISM

The analysis of the psychiatric version of violence can be advanced by comparing it with social authority, such as the "authority" of what Said (1979) called "Orientalism," that genre of authoritative texts designed to present to Westerners the mysterious East, a part of the world foreign and strange to us. Said is especially germane because he analyzes the discourse of "otherness" in the world at precisely that historical time when European and U.S. interests, both commercial and military, found it necessary to deal with "others" whose presence was no longer irrelevant to Western culture. Some understanding of the Orient was vividly necessary by the nineteenth century, when the world was one of shrinking distances and of interdependencies of commerce. Today, the same necessity is found with regard to psychopathology in our world of accelerating intrusion of puzzling, incomprehensible, and unwanted behavior among our own, behavior that nonetheless is "other" and demands that we come to a reckoning of it. Psychiatry has taken that lead, and its authority is the warrant for curing people, or failing that, removing those people who are called "schizophrenic."[3]

What Orientalist authorities did with respect to the Orient is what psychiatrists do with respect to schizophrenia.[4] In the first place, this is to assume that if schizophrenic persons could represent themselves, they would do so. Because they only puzzle and frighten us, the task of psychiatry is to represent them. Hence, second, one adopts a "strategic location" of exteriority, which assures psychiatry, and its nonschizophrenic audience, that it stands outside the psychopathology it is describing. This exteriority also allows psychiatric authority to bridge a gap. What it says builds a bridge between normal persons and mad persons so that the former can understand the latter. That bridge is a bridge of language, of text, of concepts and theory.

In authoritative texts, there is no such thing as a delivered presence,[5] but a *re-presence*, or a representation. The value, efficacy, strength, and apparent veracity of psychiatric texts therefore rely very little on, and cannot instrumentally depend on, schizophrenia in itself, as an objective "real thing." Indeed, languaged explanations of schizophrenia, or of all psychopathology, become a meaningful presence to the reader only because the explanatory texts have excluded, displaced, and made supererogatory psychopathology itself. In analyzing Orientalist authorities, Said (1979) noted:

Thus all of Orientalism stands forth and away from the Orient: that Orientalism makes sense at all depends more on the West than on the Orient, and this sense is directly indebted to various Western techniques of representation that make the Orient visible, clear, "there" in discourse about it. (p. 21)

Said concluded:

And these representations rely upon institutions, traditions, conventions, agreed-upon codes of understanding for their effects, not upon a distant and amorphous Orient. (p. 22)

Psychiatric literature, by which is meant not only the theory and technical reports written by experts for experts, but also textbooks, and advertisements for tranquilizers, for services available, and the popular treatises on how to cope with a mentally ill person in one's family—all these are in the same situation of distance from schizophrenia, and they each depend on the discourse of the reader rather than some presumably described "objective properties" of psychopathology. All such literature stands away from what it describes, and it makes sense not to patients but to normal people. Indeed, such texts assume in their audience exactly what patients are thought not to have but what normal people do, a sense of the institutions, traditions, conventions, and agreed upon codes of understanding through which people grasp the commonly accepted meanings of life.

Orientalism, as a body of literature through which Westerners know the Orient, looked at the Orient on its surface. The point of Orientalist writing over the decades has not in fact been to understand the Orient, its people, their experience, meanings, world, or life. It was to consolidate the position of the knower over against what was known, as different and superior. Psychiatric authority also looks at human suffering on its surface. Its point is not to help us to understand human suffering, the experience of sufferers, or their meanings, world, or life. It is to consolidate the position of the knower, the writer and reader, over against what is known, as different and superior.

CONCEALMENT

What is most remarkable about this intellectual situation is how thoroughly concealed it is.[6] Knowledge always conceals as it reveals, according to Heidegger, and it is important to see both sides of psychiatric knowledge.

Concealment is a crucial part of some social power, especially when that power is lodged in a profession, and that profession practices violence when it pretends not to. Efforts to legitimate that profession typically conceal the power behind claims of truth, and the accruing legitimacy becomes a means of, as well as a result of, concealment. For members of that profession, their felt truths conceal the concealment of power, yielding self-deception. In psychiatry, what may be most radically concealed is the fact that the distanced knowledge they have about their suffering clientele is geared primarily to the arena of their public, not to some scientific setting where truth is discovered. Or put more accurately, studies of neurotransmitters as "the cause" of schizophrenia falsify entirely what it is to those who know it. Schizophrenics themselves may not be able to explain why they are disturbed, but when they say that it is because of neurological events, they are repeating what they have been told. They have already lost their voice.

When, for example, psychiatric theorists say that the schizophrenic patient suffers from a genetically determined disease that affects the balance of chemicals in the brain, they are indulging a perspective that surely is legitimate. But it is also dogmatic. The disease allegedly has nothing to do with the life being led by the patient, nor the life outside the patient into which he or she is trying somehow to fit. This talk of genes and neurotransmitters may be true in a context of scientific discourse, but in terms of everyday human understanding, it is a mystification and, in fact, a claim to truth that excludes all but a small range of what the patient, and those in his or her world, must deal with. It is the same mystification that is embedded in the general notion of disease, and the even more general notion of "othering" the patient, and, finally, the ultimate dogma that there is nothing to learn from the schizophrenic patient.

This nullification of the patient, and of what we may learn from her, or what she may learn from her experiences, serves to legitimate our treatment of those we call schizophrenic, but it also serves, even less innocently, to recruit from the population more patients. By being invited to view their spiritual struggles as genetically deter-mined chemical imbalances, more people than those deeply troubled are drawn into the commercial transaction of buying psychiatric care. This does a disservice to at least some people who would be better off not nullifying their spiritual struggle, but more importantly it reinforces cultural patterns that are violent in their intolerance of human differences and human suffering. The medical roles of "patient" and "doctor" distort the space of human self-discovery and self-invention beyond recognition, and this is more true the more technological the treatment becomes.

It is important to remember at this point, that I am now speaking of institutional violence. These violations of human dignity are not the doings of individual psychiatrists; they come from traditions of professions, of science, and of medicine, which in turn are more than theories and include the roles, norms, values, procedures—in a word, the institutions of modern society. The recruitment of patients for profit, for example, is not easy to protest because most psychiatrists have to channel their activities through profit-oriented economic institutions. How could it be otherwise in modern American society?

What is revealed in this analysis is not the violence of corrupt professionals preying on innocent victims for profit. Rather it is the violence of capitalism and of technology without which much of the world we enjoy would hardly be imaginable. And yet we dare not forget this violence; only our consciousness of it, only our own realization that our modern discourses falsify as well as reveal life to us, only these ideas keep us from becoming the mad scientists of lobotomy or of Nazi experimentation.

AN EXPERT PSYCHIATRY

In 1991, Penick et al. described their treatment of major mental disorders, diagnosis-specific psychotherapy (DSP), which they offered as an improvement on previous approaches to psychotherapy.[7] I shall try to show how their approach to patients and their families moves from deeply committed efforts to help people, into a scientific dogmatism, which in turn manifests the self-deception and the concealment that lead to the violence of treatment. The psychiatry they practice is close to the very center of American psychiatry in general. Washington University in St. Louis, where they do their work, was a leader in the development of scientific diagnosis (Kirk & Kutchins, 1992) and some of its inspiration came from work done there earlier (Feighner et al., 1972).

Therefore, the efforts of these therapists are not neglectful nor mindless; they are in fact among the best efforts modern science has to offer psychotic patients. These authors have gone to extraordinary lengths to correct errors of previous schools of psychotherapy, which suffered from what they call a "scientific nihilism"—an earlier, somewhat proud, in fact, distrust of scientific method. They described these former efforts as follows:

Guesses, hunches, and speculations about why and how people become mentally ill were extracted from the diverse, multiform materials provided by people in treatment who were required to talk at length about themselves under highly permissive circumstances. These guesses, hunches, and speculations were often brilliantly woven together into tightly knit theoretical scaffolds. The same methods of observation from which these theoretical scaffolds emerged were then applied to test and confirm their theoretical validity. (p. 63)

The error cited here is a "circular reasoning" that bypasses the scientific method. "The unfortunate result is a virtual guarantee that the 'truth' of any theory of psychotherapy will be repeatedly confirmed in clinical practice." This is bad science, which led to numerous schools of psychotherapy which "flourished outside the mainstream of objective research and empirical validation."

In contrast, the authors described their method, a "psychoeducational process," that carefully works with the patient to compare his or her experiences with a systematic review of the symptoms of the major psychiatric disorders. This painstaking work with patients yields an "objectification of the illness" in three ways.

First, it maintains the patient's focus on a relatively narrow group of symptoms, concentrating the patient's attention on the essential features of his or her disorder. Occasionally patients find it difficult to provide a straightforward phenomenological description of their experiences. Instead, they offer "explanations" for their suffering rather than "accounts" of their distress. When this occurs, the DSP clinician gently but firmly asks the patient to hold off or put aside a discussion of such topics and then continues the symptom review. (pp. 54–55)

A second way in which the psychoeducational process is activated comes from the fact that this process helps stimulate patients to look for patterns and relationships:

Patients are often intensely aware of specific symptoms but are sometime surprisingly unaware of the relationships among symptoms that cluster together to form an identifiable illness. Consequently, most patients find the syndromatic review valuable because it helps them fit their pain and distress into a whole picture that has meaning. (p. 55)

Third, after this symptomatic education, family members and others attend a briefing session with the patient. There, the clinicians "with great frankness usually provide the patient with a diagnosis," along with a discussion of treatment options and realistic expectations for the course of the illness and treatment. All those present are invited to discuss these matters, to have their questions answered, and to express their feelings and concerns.

The authors are surely correct to cite flawed science in previous validations of psychotherapeutic approaches. In fact, they noted that although psychotherapy helps, "no consistent effect favoring one psychotherapy over another has been found even when psychotherapies were compared that differ greatly in their assumptions about the causes and cures of psychopathological conditions."

How can that be? Long ago, Rogers (1951) concluded from his pioneering research that the rationale and theoretical content of the different schools of psychotherapy contributed less to the "curative" process than the quality of the relationship formed between the clinician and the client. To Rogers, it was this relationship that was of special importance in helping people change, not the specific theory of causation. Over time we found ourselves partly agreeing with Rogers. It seemed to us that psychotherapists too often tried to force etiologic templates onto patients without much regard for their past and current clinical histories. (p. 63)

It is very unfortunate that these authors did not apply this sort of critique, cheerfully applied to their predecessors, to their own work. In fact, the care with which they individualize their treatment, involve the family, tutor the patient, and so on suggests they are quite aware of the effect of the relationship between them and the patient. However, they do not see themselves "forcing a template" on their patients—which in this case is a diagnostic one rather than an etiologic one. Why is some of what patients report considered an accurate "phenomenological description" of their experience, whereas other concerns are relegated to "explanations for their suffering" and postponed, not permitted, irrelevant? Indeed they may be irrelevant to criteria of the diagnosis as these are described by the profession, but they are hardly irrelevant to the patient.

Later, when syndromal clusters of symptoms are described, patients are told what goes with what to make up an "identifiable illness," but what is identifiable to professionals may differ from what is identifiable to the patient. Furthermore, they celebrate patients' coming to "fit their pain and distress into a whole picture that has meaning" but it is not the patients' meanings that count here, only the picture contained in the diagnostic template is understood as meaningful.[8] And finally, in case the psychoeducation has not been persuasive, family and others are called in for a briefing, which is a report by the experts about just what is happening in the patient's life. This report, however, eschews the patient's own explanations and forces an agreement with theirs, which is that there is an "illness" here that explains all the trouble, about which certain options exist, and so on.

However, perhaps the most important point in critique of DSP and other medicalized approaches is that it teaches the patient the distanced language of psychiatry as a way to interpret one's own symptoms. It is a discourse similar to the one to which Said called attention. It is not intended to make the symptoms intelligible in their own terms. Their own internal meanings are already assumed to be valueless, random, merely psychotic. What, therefore, patients are asked to do is to "objectify" personal struggles as "symptoms." This discourse forces them to assign their struggles to a category of otherness—elements of disease that demand nothing but to be eliminated. The mental lives of patients become objects, alien and evil diseases that have neither power nor relevance for one's life.

When we imagine the psychoeducational processes of DSP, nothing seems as similar to its cognitive process as the cognitive processes of Orientalism. It is as if we were saying:

We, the experts on things foreign and frightening, tell you, who are fearful and perhaps overwhelmed, exactly what is going on. As foreign as it is, it might seem threatening, but it is really quite quaint. See how this and that go together in their presentation. You can understand that they always do this. There is nothing here to move you beyond curiosity, or if you promise not to get too involved in them, you may be briefly fascinated.

By teaching you this, we allow you the intellectual distance from which you can master your own struggles, not so as better to participate in them and bring them to some conclusion, but rather to put them into a category with other former adversaries who, if they get close again, can be put in their place. And that place has nothing to do with you really. You, who are being helped here, are superior to your symptoms. They are an illness. Maybe they were puzzling and frightening, but now you see how they are not relevant to the more essential you, who rises above this illness by objectifying it.

Their entrance into your life is accidental. And their otherness is of course quite real. They cannot represent themselves to you in a way you can understand; if they could, then you would not be frightened and we would not have to represent them to you in terms you can understand. Now you understand them and are no longer afraid. Of course, if they get out of hand, we experts will make them go away.

AN ALTERNATIVE TO VIOLENCE

This frame of meaning, imposed by experts, is preliminary to eliminating the symptom, which may be done (most frequently recently) by medication, or (more often earlier) by electroshock or lobotomy. Even if there were a "magic bullet" technology that could simply eliminate incorrect thoughts, some framing like DSP would be necessary in order for the patient to settle for giving up whatever was meaningful or seductive about the symptom.

This "strategy" is very clear in DSP, but it is built into all medicalized interpretations of psychoses like schizophrenia. And although such medical thinking has been around a long time, it has never been the only way to understand psychosis. An alternative half a century ago was Boison (1955), who like Sullivan (1940, 1962), Arieti (1955), and others, insisted that the struggle of psychosis is about something—something important in one's life, one's narrative flow of self, which always remembers where it came from and worries where it is going.

Boison, for example, argued that "certain forms of mental illness are themselves manifestations of healing power."[9] He acknowledged, of course, that such cases have to be distinguished from others. Other patients have adapted to defeat, and they have invested their social career, and their personal identity, in being a "psychiatric" patient. In such cases, it is practically impossible to mobilize once again the redeeming power of the original struggle. And yet Boison believes that it would be a grave error to reduce the personal crisis to a mere disease.

Some psychotic breaks, especially in late adolescence, are periods of personal reorganization so profound that space, time, and identity become confused. For most individuals, however, such reorganizations usually take place in small steps, in dreams and superficial changes that are not remarkable. But there are, in some people's lives, times when reorganizations are sudden and disorienting. The difference between such cases is a difference of many factors that have to do with one's personal history, one's accrued style of handling conflicts and confusions, as well as the urgency that is propelled by some current demand, internal or external.

Other psychotic breaks have clear reference to contemporary stresses and crises that draw on otherwise quiet sources of unrest and propulsion in order to reorganize the self. Yet others, such as the "negative symptoms" of "process schizophrenia," are very slow and insidious, hardly transitional at all. A crisis seems current (instead of chronic) only because earlier, more beginning stages were lost track of in the development of negative symptoms, lost amid other traits to which the person and those around him or her had become accustomed.

Boison also noted that the delusions and hallucinations of acute psychotic episodes often have religious content. In fact, he is eager to

frankly acknowledge that religion is associated with mental illness . . . [that it is] concerned with that which is not yet and ought to be, both in personal character and social order. . . . It is ever religion's task to disturb the conscience of men [*sic*] regarding the quality of the life they are living and the failure to achieve their true potentialities. (p. 41)

Still, schizophrenia is not easy to deal with. Active symptoms like anxiety, self-blame, or restlessness may be referred back to the personal crisis from which they come. More passive symptoms like withdrawal and concealment are naturally more difficult to interpret. The first kind of symptoms motivates action in the world, which is a place where feedback from both others and nature can be corrective. In contrast, the psychic interior of withdrawal is a space with more possibilities for genuine innovation, either sane or insane. In psychotic withdrawal, the innovations may not yield to social influences without a protracted struggle. Nevertheless, Boison followed Hutchinson (1943) in seeing a similarity among religious, artistic, and scientific insights, and in an article in *Psychiatry* Boison (1947) explored how these each are like and different from a schizophrenic break.

CONCLUSIONS

Taking the Boison position seriously, along with the similarity between psychiatric discourse and Orientalism, we must conclude that important parts of what is called psychopathology are neglected, that these parts engage moral and spiritual (as opposed to chemical and anatomical) matters, and that this neglect comes from how practitioners shape with language their attempt to help schizophrenic patients. This sort of analysis appears elsewhere, as in Herman and Kemper (1993), who also argued that scientific discourse is not the same discourse as that in terms of which ordinary people grasp the exigencies of their lives:

the conceptual system of the psychologist as a scientist has become so prevailing over the conceptual system of the subject that there has not been much room left for the expression of the voice of the individual person as a knowledgeable individual.

To take the schizophrenic seriously as a knowledgeable individual is to do what one can to avoid violence, and it is also to avoid neglecting aspects of psychopathology not codified in science. Boison is developmental in much of his thinking, and the process of cognitive development contains ways of dealing with moral questions as well as factual ones. Psychological theories and research about the acquisition of factual knowledge are quite detailed; the theory of the acquisition of moral questioning is less so. And yet, there are no cases of psychopathology in my clinical experience that do not have, at or near their very center, questions like "Who am I supposed to be? What should I do? What is good? What is right? Whose opinion must I honor?" and so on—all moral issues.

Furthermore, in severe pathology like schizophrenia, these questions, and their answers, are often formulated metaphorically, clung to desperately, and struggled with continuously. Indeed, the discourse of the psychotic may be quite opaque, and yet the opaqueness is relieved somewhat by seeing its moral dimension. Every child grows up with preoccupations about the "right thing to do" or the "right person to be." These are as fully important to psychiatry and psychology as the more typical information that populates our cognitive studies.

Moral and spiritual matters were there for all of us to deal with, as children, adolescents, and adults. That dealing was often not easy. If one has experienced contradictory demands, unbearable loneliness, repeated abandonment, traumatic losses, heartless exploitation, and cold neglect, these questions become both more urgent and less answerable. Beliefs will become shaped by the need for answers; behavior patterns will become detached from beliefs, feelings will be mystified, and psychopathology will be born.

To the extent that the experience of a schizophrenic person is comprehensible at all, the discourse will have to take up such spiritual questions. These questions are sometimes moral in the sense of social morality; often they are religious and transcendental. The psychiatric neglect of such things in psychiatry's own belief system is no excuse for neglecting them in the lives of our patients, whom science presumably wants to understand. Not doing so manifests exactly the "exteriority" Said revealed in Orientalism. The institutional violence born of Orientalism bears, not accidentally, similarities to the institutional violence perpetrated every day against schizophrenic persons.

If we are serious about changing violence against patients, we shall have to overcome the neglect, in psychology and psychiatry, of those spiritual struggles that characterize their lives. We shall have to see the partiality of scientific discourse; we shall have to target the way institutional use of that discourse becomes violent; we shall have to overcome psychiatric dogmatism. Furthermore, we shall have to learn again about spirituality,[10] indeed we shall have to embrace it as the arena capable of preventing the violence born of dogmatism in the science and contempt in the practice.

Left over from earlier times, every state hospital has at least one chaplain. His or her position is nearly always marginal within the power relations of the staff. Chaplains may be allowed to work with patients, but their role is understood to be very specialized and specific. This is ironic, for spirituality is not only religious, nor is it, finally, somehow "mental" and separate from embodied persons. Spirituality is near the center of schizophrenic struggles, it is an important feature of humanity. It is time for it to be an important feature of psychology and psychiatry.

Moving to the larger argument, the depersonalization in DSP is a case of objectification, which in itself may not be an error. But this objectification progresses to violence insofar as the inner life of the individual is depersonalized and cast in the role of disease, an evil process that has no right to exist. Suffering should be relieved, and psychiatry sometimes does this. But we also see vivid examples of professional reification of our own diagnostic categories, and of projecting into them the evil that gives our work and our lives the cast of goodness.

These are larger, institutional processes that have nourished psychopharmacology and protected it from criticism. Given the institutional and cultural context at the beginning of the twenty first century, no psychiatrist can avoid objectifying and depersonalizing her or his patients with medication. The treatment professions have become efforts to alienate persons from their symptoms in an effort to bring them back into the fold. Patients are to agree with their practitioners and reject their own lives; that is the price of acceptance. As professionals, practitioners do not for a minute suppose that anything in the patients' "disease" may be informative. Symptoms seem to reveal nothing about ourselves or our culture, and our hasty refusal to listen to it practically guarantees that we will not learn from patients' experiences or our own.

These failures of treatment are not individual failures by particular professionals as much as they are issues for the entire profession, for the culture of science in which it has embedded itself, and for how the profession has come to reckon legitimacy. It is arresting to contemplate the possibility that our violence and our legitimacy come from the same place.

NOTES

1. Lifton (1997) suggested that those who presided over Nazi death camps underwent a psychological process, similar to dissociation, which he called *doubling*. This process enabled them to do their Nazi job while, during the evenings, they lived happily with their families. "In sum, doubling is the psychological means by which one invokes the evil potential of the self" (p. 35). The term *evil* may be more judgmental than some may think is appropriate for this book, but I have seen some version of doubling in those who apply electroshock therapy.

2. Bulhan's (1985) book is about Franz Fanon, whose life and work dealt simultaneously with psychiatry, racism, and violence. Bulhan demystified this somewhat legendary figure, but along the way made clear that the violence of the civilized West in this century is one of the most impressive in history.

3. Representing schizophrenics to family and hospital staff often feels like advocacy, clarifying to these constituencies the needs and intentions of the victims of schizophrenia. Anyone who has done this work is inevitably tempted to pretend to understand more than is possible. These constituencies often want practitioners to understand schizophrenia, so that they can help *them*, as well as the schizophrenics, with their pain. Many practitioners are familiar with the temptations of apparent wisdom in this setting, but Said made clear other temptations—if not inevitabilities—in this role.

4. For example, Feighner et al. (1972) laboriously worked out the procedures for collecting the data for psychiatric diagnosis. Although the decisions they made were necessary decisions for the research as they understood it, it is also clear that their understanding had little to do with the patient's understanding, and much to do with understanding that professionals routinely have.

5. An effort to make accessible the presence, rather than merely to represent, schizophrenia had a final appearance in Laing in the 1960s. Its disappearance is more than a loss of respect for the patients' own point of view. It is a loss of crucial insights into their—and the practitioner's—functioning as professionals try, sometimes despairingly, to get through a mental hospital day; c.f. Laing, R. D. (1967, 1971).

6. Concealment by psychiatry from the public and from itself is taken up in detail in my analysis of psychiatric power (see Keen, 1998, chap. 8).

7. Some of this material has appeared earlier in Keen (1998, chap. 9).

8. Of course, this treatment team knows what reality is, and that knowing dictates that deviations from their perception are simply part of the illness. If professionals are told by the patient that they do not understand their (the patient's) experience, or that they (the treatment professionals) are merely gathering evidence for calling them crazy, the perspicacity of this remark is dismissed, apparently on the strength of the well-defined and consensual status as "treatment personelle," as opposed to mere "patients." The practicality of this understanding may be apparent to professionals; it feels unjust to patients.

9. This sentence is from Boison (1955, p. 41).

10. It is with ambivalence that I use the term *spirituality*. My fears are that either I will say too little for those who have developed it, or that mentioning it at all is saying too much for the remainder of readers.

chapter 8

QUESTIONING PSYCHOLOGICAL MODERNITY

PSYCHOLOGICAL MODERNITY

Modernity referred to the nineteenth century in the nineteenth century, to the twentieth century in the twentieth, and so on. The term says "now" and evokes a context of historical flow, centuries long. To call modernity questionable is to say that "now," the current historical period, can be questioned. Indeed, it should be questioned with respect to the wisdom of what one is doing, and my part of that questioning here is in psychology, with a particular focus on clinical psychology.

Modernity must be questioned from within it. Since I too am situated historically, my approach speaks about that situating foisted on me by the accident of having been born in this century. Furthermore, I begin this conclusion explicitly autobiographically.

When I was a graduate student, I was at war with B. F. Skinner and John Watson, the two U.S. psychologists who defined behaviorism and shaped the discipline as we have had it in the twentieth century. My war was not a private one; there were other dissenters. What bothered me, however, was not the tenuousness of the knowledge.

These scientists had made it possible for psychology to know things with the certainty of science, and that science was a lot more certain than, say, the sort of psychology that William James had been able to accomplish in 1890.

My complaint, therefore, was that in giving in to the appeal to certainty and science in defining our field, we limited ourselves to studying only those things that could be known this way. Behaviorism was like a reduction of psychology to physics. This was very different from William James, whose reflectiveness and speculation had, in Watson and Skinner, given way to a more aggressive technological mentality. In their psychologies, certainty was essential if results were to be had. We see here, then, the beginning of my questioning of modernity. What psychologists called "results" were ironically shaped by James' own pragmatism; results were the ability to do something and know ahead of time what would happen. If I reward a behavior, it will increase in frequency. If I ignore it and prevent reward from following it, it will decrease in frequency.

I have referred to this sense of results as *technology*. Technical expertise is applied to concrete problems, and solutions are found. Watson and Skinner promised, and delivered, such results. In contrast, the questions that preoccupied James, such as what to do, what goals to aim for with technological power, how goals operate in human consciousness, disappeared from the field. But in addition, all accompanying issues, such as who should decide what should be done, were not a part of behaviorist psychology.[1]

In behaviorism, dealing with people, helping them, changing them, were approached in the same way as controlling any other part of nature. For example, in Skinner's shaping students' behavior so as to maximize learning, *what was learned* was not an issue in the science of psychology. Even more egregiously, the person learning did not chose what to learn. Thus, human agency was not part of psychological theory. Not only James, but Thorndike (1903), Angell (1904), and many others would have been horrified.

The assumed and unexplored agent in behaviorism is the behaviorist scientist. This was a technological science; a part of the larger modern project of mastering nature. Persons who learned or were otherwise affected by behaviorist certainties were seen as a part of nature. Nature became the Great Object, including human life itself, over against the Great Subject, natural science.[2] Such a format for psychology followed patterns already laid down in medicine, where the human body was found to yield to manipulation by technology in curing disease, prolonging life, and so on. It was hard to be against such technology in the early 1960s, when I was a graduate student. I held out, but without much certainty. Certainty was the property of science.

I had only questions to offer, but of course, that was enough to be a psychology professor. It was also enough to be a psychotherapist, whose job is less technological and more a matter of asking questions than answering them. Psychotherapy does not bring answers. It is not analogous to medical cure. So my war with behaviorism continued, but it became a larger matter of questioning the sort of science that based its legitimacy in practical success. For practical success involved mastering nature in American science, and mastering nature was itself coming into question in its technological excesses. By now, the beginning of the twenty-first century, the ecological crisis has become vivid enough to confirm the importance of the questions that I felt had been left out of psychology.

FROM JAMES TO ECOLOGY[3]

Using William James as a model, I state these questions now again, hoping less to answer them than to ask them successfully. The goal of successful asking is exactly uncertain, for I do not know what will happen. This pattern is a vivid contrast to science, to behaviorism, and to the project of mastering nature. The technological project listens to nature respond so as better to master it. Mastering itself is not questioned. Asking a question in my sense, in contrast, seeks a future of continuing dialogue, with unpredictable results. In asking a question like "What should be done?" I am creating a dialectical process, like a conversation.

A conversation, as noted in chapter 6, meanders through two landscapes of the mental lives of the two parties conversing. Together they create a common, overlapping, verbal landscape, built on a prior common culture but unique in its particular dynamics and content. A conversation creates a common world within the larger one, and the direction of wandering through it has no constraints beyond the questions and answers of the conversing pair. The unpredictability is exactly characteristic of a dialectical process as opposed to technological mastery. The science behind technology tests hypotheses one at a time for the benefit of scientific understanding, and for the application of that understanding technologically to control outcomes with as little uncertainty as possible.

Some science converses dialectically with nature; James' psychology was like that. The "psyche," the human mind, was the object to be studied and to be enriched by such study. From having undergone this enrichment, it can better ask more questions and learn more. The "object" of this science is itself a subject. Between the scientist and his or her subject matter is an exchange in which both benefit.

In contrast, technological science masters nature.[4] We are, as parties to the Great Technological Subject, all beneficiaries, but nature is not. Nature learns nothing from us. We grant it no right to know us, and we grant it no right to instruct us in defining what we should do.

In a dialectic like a conversation, the other becomes known to me and I become known to the other. We cannot do physics and chemistry that way, for the physical world cannot know us in any meaningful sense. But we certainly can do psychology that way. However, to see the other as an object of nature, which does not itself know, is to cut the dialectic in half. We know our objects in behaviorism, but they do not know us. And because an object is known, but is not a knower, it has nothing to teach us from its point of view. Hence we listen only for what we want to hear. We do not listen to what the other wants us to know, for it is assumed ahead of time, by the behaviorist subject, that this other, an object, does not have a perspective from which we can learn.[5]

Neglecting to take seriously the feedback from nature in our ecological crisis is only the first step in suffering the consequences of our own technology. Having no desire to be known by nature, of course, makes sense to us. Nature does not "know," in the view of technological science. Nature is an object; it is known. We, and only we, are knowers. Nature is ours, it belongs to us. We do not belong to it, and hence we owe it no regard beyond our own goals.

The present "crisis" in ecology is the last step in suffering the consequences of our own technology. Between the first step, of neglecting to take seriously that integrity that suffers the impact of our technology, and the last step, which is to realize that we depend on that integrity, that we do belong to nature, that it does have an existence and an integrity of its own that we must respect—between this first and last step in the technological progress of modernity lies exactly—science in its technological rather than dialectical mode.

This ecological diversion in the discussion validates the resistance I felt as a graduate student to the mindlessness of behaviorism. I had an attitude toward persons, who are known by psychology, that was a kind of respect, or even reverence. If anything was "sacred" to me, it was persons. In the present context of the ecological crisis, we now wonder whether we ought not see nature with different eyes. Is it sacred? At least we must treat it with respect if not with reverence. And to respect or pay homage to nature is to do more than scientific knowing. It is to engage a different enterprise from technological mastery. It is to engage an enterprise different from science. It is to listen to what nature tells us of its own priorities, it is to respect them, and to submit to them as constraints which we call moral.

As the psychology of the twentieth century concludes itself in a burst of technological mastery, including psychopharmacology, we see the unconscious frenzy of such technological manipulation in an entirely new and frightening guise. Even though this mastery is a much more direct assault on the integrity of nature as it is given, we continue here to neglect the nonscientific, that is, the moral, question.

FROM ECOLOGY TO PSYCHOPHARMACOLOGY

It is science fiction, in a way, to suppose that human problems can be solved with pills, and even as we indulge this scientific fantasy with our practice, we are engaging profound moral questions without recognizing that we are doing so. It is our preoccupation with the scientific, of course, that masks the moral content of the science itself. Our hubris and arrogance that technology can improve not only our material conditions but also our mental ones blind us to the moral content of the new area we have technologically created. We can control the rougher edges of human experience. With enormous self-congratulation, we trim the tragedy of human existence as we find it, and we reduce the strenuousness of human life itself, down to a size that is within what students have taught me to call our "comfort zone."

This is an idolatrous act, this playing God by technologically lopping off the unpleasantness of life, going far beyond our sickness and hunger all the way to our sadness and our fears, our loneliness and our terror of death. In order to play this existential game with the tools of science, we must pretend that what we are doing is something else (such as treating diseases).

Such pretending has been well-known in the twentieth century. The atomic bomb vastly expanded our power of life and death. This degree of killing plays God, too, and thus must also pretend that it is not about doing that, not about our human smallness in the face of the mystery of life. We pretended instead that atomic war was about defeating communism—or in the case of the Soviet atomic program, it was supposed to be about the defeat of capitalism.

The cold war was about many things, such as national pride and economic greed. However, the pretenses, the ideological cloak, covered with thin rationalization the intolerance we have for our frailty, among other things, in the face of life as we find it. In order to preserve this self-deception, we have also disguised for ourselves our reasons to master more and more. We tell ourselves that it develops our moral courage and stamina, and our ability to rise to the occasion of facing the increasingly complex and difficult challenges of the morality of technology itself. But in fact, our effort is sometimes merely to indulge our greed, or, more commonly, to quell our fears that human survival is threatened until such strength and mastery are within our grasp.

So it is the unspoken moral import of technology, of the psychopharmacological project in particular, that most fascinates me. And this fact brings into focus another—that helping people through psychotherapy, or any intervening in lives of others as psychologists at all, has always been a moral enterprise. That too is rarely taught because we use the language of science in psychology—a language that makes our effort more efficient in its practical power but also a language that conceals from us these moral spaces within which psychology so proudly practices.

In psychopharmacology, the technology becomes more powerful, convenient, and reliable—or if that is not quite true, with modern mental drugs we can at least say that the hope of such a technological mastery of the human soul can more convincingly be entertained. In a culture like ours that worships technology, it is a short step to realize that we are worshipping our own power. If we care to, we can see the extremity of our ambition, and then the questionable moral character of other technologies, come into focus. More than any other technology, psychopharmacology shows us our folly.

I have already made it clear that there are situations where drugs work very well, facilitating human struggles with tragedy, without eliminating pain, and unhappiness, and tragedy. If we can see what we are doing without automatically medicalizing human suffering, without transforming human unhappiness into a disease to be technologically fixed, then the moral issues are visible.

Paying attention to the questions embedded in all psychopathology—"Who am I to become?"—should be the constant framework within which all psychological help is received. That is the key psychological question for all of us, no matter how we become disturbed, or how disturbed we become.[6]

Short of this rarely mentioned moral context for pharmacological treatment, the project of psychopharmacological help masquerades as science and medicine, safely contained by the traditions and ideologies of healing and cure, and its moral content is obscured. Thus also, because of this obscuring, we propose to be technologists, and thus we practice technology's worst hubris and arrogance.

IS PSYCHOPHARMACOLOGY IMMORAL?

Is it immoral to make life a little better with a little Prozac? Or for that matter, with a little whiskey? The two traditions, of alcohol consumption and the taking of medicine, are very different. Each offers meanings to the act of chemically altering one's experience; each offers different meanings, although the act bears inescapable similarities.

Unlike a prohibitionist, I am not categorically against making life a little better through chemistry. But I am very much against doing so in the spirit of technology, the project of mastering nature. Psychopharmacology is usually practiced as a technology like laser surgery. The patient merely follows orders and receives the treatment. The operator is the doctor who seeks, with technology, to change the contours of the patient's experience. The doctor calls it "medicine," "healing," "mastering the nature" of the patient's unmastered mental life. And individuals pay many dollars for these cures.

As a patient who asks for and gets such chemical fixes for his or her mental troubles, is the patient really any different from a customer in a bar? Alcohol has, of course, a lousy reputation; it creates addictions that destroy marriages, homes, and lives. Prozac may well save marriages, homes, and lives. The cases seem very different. But are they? I know of alcoholics who drink in order to hurt their spouses and families. I also know of Prozac takers who flaunt their cheerful mood as a way to ignore the pleading of spouse and family, who declare their medical privilege as destructively as those alcoholics who use alcohol not only to spite their spouses but to negate the spouses' messages, to nullify the feedback of the interpersonal environment.

That these things happen in alcoholism is well known. That they happen in psychopharmacology is not, perhaps because psychopharmacology is rarer than drinking, and perhaps because this use of medical drugs may be rarer than this use of alcohol. Is it also possible that these uses of tranquilizers and antidepressants are seen less frequently because practitioners automatically invoke a medical context instead of a moral one? Once a chemical is officially identified as "medicine," it is automatic to look for the reduction of suffering or the cure of a disease, in a person called "a patient." The drinking man or woman is not a patient, but is "a drunk." Could these prior definitions, a *patient* and a *drunk*, define for us what we think we see?

Because Prozac is the second best-selling pharmaceutical product of all prescription drugs in any drug store, it would seem that it would be known by now if this drug were as destructive as alcohol—of relationships, of families, of lives. Indeed it is not so. But the difference is relative. Both intervene chemically in the mind of one who is unhappy and eliminates that unhappiness chemically. If the elimination of such unhappiness is not morally questionable in the case of Prozac, why is it usually believed to be so in the case of alcohol?

Aside from the different categories into which these two drugs are put, an answer is that alcohol is a much clumsier drug, much less efficient. It makes one feel better only temporarily, and it improves one's behavior only temporarily, after which it makes its user into a person more miserable, as well as spreading misery for others. And finally, after extended use, *not* using it has all these bad effects as well. Alcohol is a very crude approximation of Aldous Huxley's "soma" in *Brave New World*. Prozac is more precise. It may lessen one's sensitivity to the unhappiness one should feel, but it lacks the long-term effects of addiction. Prozac is much improved alcohol.

That still does not make it medicine. Prozac is medicine only to the extent that unhappiness is disease. We may believe we can discriminate unhappiness that is a disease from unhappiness that is not a disease, but this is a slippery issue indeed. It should be viewed as unlikely, for example, that the patients whose $1.83 billion spent on Prozac in 1997 all experienced a change from disease to health. What they experienced was more happiness, much as if they had found a much improved cocktail.

So if we decide that it is a mistake to call Prozac "a medicine" in some of those $1.83 billion worth of pills, we still cannot say that it is immoral to use it. Is it immoral to be happy, even if the happiness is chemically induced? When it does not produce addiction (some tranquilizers do so), it is hard to say just when it is and when it is not immoral. We certainly must suspect that it sometimes is, for sometimes we should be unhappy. Sometimes our sense of "something wrong," even when it is vague and haunting, is speaking a truth, and to ignore such unhappiness by negating it chemically shuts down our own moral equipment, and makes us insensitive to life's moral nuances, perhaps to our own moral failures.[7]

None of this establishes that psychopharmacology is immoral. But it does argue that we may, in our less tortured self-doubts, ourselves become less moral when we use it. I cannot quite, however, simply stop there. There are also, no doubt, cases where increased happiness and reduced grumpiness make us more moral. Here, psychopharmacology is not immoral. Like all technology, it is neutral in itself. Atomic energy may be used to save or destroy populations. Pharmacology may be used to enhance or reduce our humane sensitivities. Psychopharmacologists do not, however, announce these matters. They do not explore, or ask their patients to explore, the central human question of all of us: Who am I to become?

Despite all these considerations, however, it is inescapable that the conditions of life for our grandchildren will be different from ours, and this particular difference will engage not only the conditions of life that we experience around us. It will engage the conditions of our experience of life around us.

We all want our children and grandchildren to experience a world with less injustice. Psychopharmacology may reduce the injustices of the world, but it will not necessarily enhance our sensitivity to them. By eliminating the painful fringe of neurotic suffering, we also risk eliminating moral qualms. In fact, we have considerable difficulty telling the difference between neurotic suffering and moral qualms, and we have even more difficulty admitting that this is true.

ANTICIPATING THE FUTURE

When a society and a culture have difficulty discriminating moral qualms from neurotic suffering, any technology that reduces the sensitivities of human consciousness risks eliminating both in the spirit of mastering nature. We may proudly eliminate what we call "neurosis," which is, in our lexicon, a "disease." It is hard to be against this project. But my fear is that this medicine has side effects not yet taken into account, side-effects more serious than the dry mouth, constipation, and sexual dysfunction that accompany the use of some antidepressants. What does it do to our experience, exactly? Is our judgment about that better than that of the incipient alcoholic?

In the larger picture, the human brain evolved in such a way that we maximize the chances of our survival. Mastery of nature was a requirement for surviving floods and famine, pestilence, and disease. These technical capabilities have been extended to relieving the stresses we have created with modernity. Some of these stresses signal problems that need our attention. Some of these problems are called "moral," others "tragedy." It is possible that eliminating our openness to tragedy, dulling our capability for feeling the pain of others, muting outrage at social injustice, and curing our ruminative and compulsive need to worry about what we are bequeathing to our grandchildren— it is possible that these capabilities are here for a reason, and that we should not eliminate them? Maybe they serve us well.

But so far, our hedonic and our prideful tendencies, and perhaps our fearfulness, have governed our use of psychopharmacology. I worry that this does not serve our grandchildren well.

NOTES

1. I do not want to imply that American psychology and psychiatry have ignored consciousness altogether. Tolman (1932), himself a behaviorist (although a renegade), tried to include goals and consciousness in behavioral studies of rat maze learning. In addition, phenomenological psychology has for years put consciousness in the very center of psychology (e.g., see Valle & King, 1978; Valle & von Eckartsberg, 1981). Of course phenomenological psychology remains a philosophically sophisticated but popularly marginal branch of American psychology. For an introduction, see Keen (1975). Additionally, cognitive theories of behavior, therapy, and information processing offer limited but important modifications, as noted in chapter 3.

2. Perhaps a number of nonbehaviorist psychologists, and also psychiatrists, insofar as they practice psychotherapy, are exceptions to this statement.

3. There are many good books on the environment and its current crisis. I recommend particularly the relatively recent Morrison (1995). In thinking about these issues, I have learned from my friend Douglas, Sturm (1998), that we can distinguish the following four degrees of involvement with the natural world as an object of our attention: consumerism, conservation, environmentalism, and ecology. Each pronounces an ethic for the regulation of our treatment of nature, which are, respectively, instrumentalism, future indulgence, aesthetic appreciation, and existential connection and interpenetration. As we move from instrumentalism to connection and

interpenetration results in experiencing an increasing "caring for" or "involvement with" or "reverence toward" nature, as the natural world approaches the status of the sacred.

4. Mastery of nature is a very general project. A culture has such projects, themes that make its way of life distinctive. Medieval monks did many things, but everything they did was a part of the larger, more general project of glorifying God. The Romans conquered land and extended the benefit of the Empire to all it touched. The Kwakiutl Indians (Benedict, 1934) struggled for supremacy in prestige within their community, and everything each of them did, if not in the service of this common project, at least could not contradict it and had to be deemed advisable, or not, in light of these stakes. Much of the ethos of each culture explicitly serves such definitions of what is good, what the purpose of life is.

In the Western world at the turn of the millennium, mastering nature is a project simply assumed to be good by everyone. We all are fascinated by the Human Genome Project that seeks to master the genetic code; fields like immunology increasingly manipulate the immune system in the service of increasing its efficiency in defeating such diseases as cancer. The sciences of engineering increasingly remake the environment into a product of our desire, to transform an adversary into a replica of our own vision. There are aesthetic, moral, and other projects, but mastery of nature is indeed a very large one for Americans and those around the globe whom we influence.

Psychopharmacology does not advertise itself often as a part of the project of mastering nature, but it clearly is that. Like all such projects, joining its effort, or even enjoying its results, enlists us in a definition of what life is for. We do not tell ourselves this is what we are doing very often, although no one who benefits from a psychotropic drug is very far from such a realization. We may tell ourselves that these pills help me to get along with my family, but we are never far from appreciating their help in terms of confidence and pride at how nature may play its tricks but that we are gaining a definitive edge in an adversarial relationship.

Like the ultimate prestige of the Kwakiutl, or the ultimate glorification of God for the medieval monk, we do not often ask whether the mastery of nature is a good idea, or at what point such a project would be done, or whether such mastery leaves us with nothing left of nature but an extension of our own imagination and intelligence. Such projects do not ask us such questions; they answer such questions and ask of us only how we are going to do our personal bit to help.

5. This description of behavioristic psychology, and its contrast to the dialectic, will remind some of a central difference between Aristotle and Plato (or Socrates). Aristotle focused on the world, of nature, politics, art—

whatever his *object* was, and he may have asked and listened, and learned through conversation, but the defining act of knowledge was to write, which is to display the information for a reader. Like the positivist scientist, what is known is known as an object, which means both that it is known "objectively" and that it is "objectified."

Positivist knowing is codified in language for another, and that language is to be read like an instruction book. If you want to check what I know for yourself, my language objectively codes operations for you to follow in order to see what I saw and to know what I know. Aristotle certainly was less "operational" in his definitions, but the spirit is the same. A writer is responsible for his content. It is his version of truth. It emerges from many sources, but it definitely is not the joint product of an interaction between two poles of a dialectic.

In contrast, Plato's dialogues do not codify knowledge in a catalogue of abstractions, arranged hierarchically. They end, but they do not conclude, for there is always another dialogue to have about the same topic. Knowledge emerges from the space between people, a space where each is visible to the other, as a person with an angle of vision, a personal history and a perspective. To know about something is to know what someone else has known, but modified by what I bring to it from a perspective slightly (or greatly) different from my dialogical counterplayer. We exchange our versions, influence one another, pool our knowledge, appreciate the differences of our perspectives even as we also appreciate what we share, never believing that what we share is the last word, because there are other perspectives to appreciate.

Behaviorism, and other positivisms, including science in general, is Aristotelian and not Socratic. Why it eventuates in a mastery of nature is related to the objectification of its subject matter. If the other that is known is an object, and I am a subject, I transcend it. Dialectical knowledge, on the other hand, involves being known, and I appreciate knowing the other and being known, for we generate together what I know. I can't do it alone; the other is not my object, so I do not seek to master it. Even what we talk about, while objectified, is never fully mastered. If it has a point of view, I am obliged to listen.

6. This formulation, like much of the philosophical background of this book, is existential. Heidegger (1927/1962) insisted that a person's existence is "at issue" for that person. That is, how to live, who to become, who to die having been—these questions, while often implicit, are characteristic for all human beings, and, I submit, are at the center of all those troubles we call *psychopathology*. This formulation does not negate Freud's, or Beck's, or Rogers', or even Bandura's formulations, but it definitely "reframes" these

in terms I have consistently found to be germane to the experience of psychotherapy. This is true especially for the identified patient, but not only for that person.

7. I sometimes entertain the fantasy that we will some day solve both the problem of overprescription and the problem of the maldistribution of drugs so that those who really need them the most are the ones to get them. Suppose this happens, and we trim off the suffering of those who suffer the most without indulging hedonic avoidances. What would technology have done, and what would we have done? Because we would have defined our psychopharmacological efforts as "treating diseases," we would thus have made even more obvious the fact that after the disease is cured, what remains is to live life. This in turn presses upon us once again, as individual persons and as a community, questions that lie beneath the creation of symptoms in the first place, such as "Who are we to become?" This sort of question then evolves into issues of justice and art, two enterprises that do not at their center yield to technological solutions. Only human decisions now count, not technological mastery. If this is our future, why not start now with such questions, of "the good, the true, and the beautiful," with which we are condemned to deal eventually anyway if our lives are to have meaning?

References

Ader, R., Felten, D. L., & Cohen, N. (Eds.). (1991). *Psychoneuro-immunology*. New York: Academic Press.

Alexander, F. (1943). Fundamental concepts of psychosomatic research: Psychogenesis, Conversion, Specificity. *Psychosomatic. Medicine*, V, 1943, 1–109.

Alexander, F. (1950). *Psychosomatic medicine*. New York: Norton.

Angell, J. R. (1904). *Psychology*. New York: Henry Holt.

Anscombe, R. (1987). The disorder of consciousness in schizophrenia. *Schizophrenia Bulletin*, *13*, 241–260.

Arieti, S. (1955). *Interpretation of schizophrenia*. New York: Brunner.

Azima, H. (1961). Psychodynamic and psychotherapeutic problems in connection with imipramine intake. *Journal of Mental Science*, *197*, 74.

Baxter, R. L., Schwartz, J. M., Bergman, K. S., Szuba, M. P., Guze, B. H., Marriotta, J. C., Alazvaki, A., Selin, C. E., Feung, H. K., Munford, P., & Phelps, M. E. (1992). Caudate glucose metabolic rate changes with both drug and behavior therapy for obsessive-compulsive disorder. *Archives of General Psychiatry*, *49*, 681–689.

Beck, A. (1967). *Depression: Clinical, experimental, and theoretical aspects*. New York: Harper & Row.

Beitman, B., & Klerman, G. L. (Eds.). (1991). *Integrating pharmacotherapy and psychotherapy*. Washington, DC: American Psychiatric Press.

Bell, M. (1985). *The turkey shoot: Tracking the Attica coverup*. New York: Grove Press.

Benedict, R. (1934). *Patterns of culture*. Boston: Houghton Mifflin.

Birley, J., & Brown, G. W. (1970). Crisis and life changes preceding the onset or relapse of acute schizophrenia: Clinical aspects. *British Journal of Psychiatry*, *16*, 327–333.

Blackstock, N. (1975). *Cointelpro: The FBI's secret war on political freedom*. New York: Vintage.

Boison, A. T. (1947). Onset in acute schizophrenia. *Psychiatry*, *10*, 159–166,

Boison, A. T. (1955). *Religion in crisis and custom: A sociological and psychological study*. New York: Harper.

Boring, E. G. (1950). *A history of experimental psychology.* New York: Appleton-Century-Crofts.

Breggin, P. R. (1991). *Toxic psychiatry: Why therapy, empathy, and love must replace the drugs, electroshock, and biochemical theories of the "new psychiatry."* New York: St. Martin's Press.

Breggin, P. R. (1994). *Talking back to Prozac; What doctors aren't telling you about today's most controversial drug.* New York: St. Martin's Press.

Brown, P., & Funk, S. C. (1986). Tardive dyskinesia: Barriers to the professional recognition of an iatrogenic disease. *Journal of Health and Social Behavior, 27,* 116–132.

Broyard, A. (1992). *Intoxicated by my illness.* New York: Fawcett Columbine.

Bulhan, H. A. (1985). *Franz Fanon and the psychology of oppression.* New York: Plenum Press.

Caplan, R. B. (1969). *Psychiatry and community in nineteenth-century America.* New York: Basic Books.

Castillo, R. J. (1996). *Culture and mental illness: A client-centered approach.* Pacific Grove, CA: Brooks/Cole.

Chouinard, G., Annable, L., & Ross-Chouinard, A. (1986). Supersensitivity psychosis and tardive dyskinesia: A survey in schizophrenic outpatients. *Psychopharmacology Bulletin, 22,* 891–896.

Chouinard, G., & Jones, B. D. (1980). Neuroleptic-induced supersensitivity psychosis: Clinical and pharmacologic characteristics. *American Journal of Psychiatry, 137,* 16–21.

Cleaver, K. (1994). Philadelphia fire. *Peace Review, 5*(4), 467–474.

Cole, J. O., & Klerman, G. L. (1964). Phenothiazine treatment in acute schizophrenia. *Archives of General Psychiatry, 10,* 246–261.

Cooper, D. E. (1990). *Existentialism.* Oxford, UK: Blackwell.

Damasio, A. R. (1994). *Descartes' error: Emotion, reason, and the human brain.* New York: Avon.

Degen, K., & Nasper, E. (1996). *Return from madness: Psychotherapy with people taking the new antipsychotic medications and emerging from severe, lifelong, and disabling schizophrenia.* Northvale, NJ: Jason Aronson.

de M'Uzan, N. (1974). Psychodynamic mechanisms in psychosomatic symptom formation. *Psychotherapy of Psychosomatics, 23,* 103–110.

Dobash, R. E., & Dobash, R. P. (1979). *Violence against wives: A case against patriarchy.* New York: The Free Press.

Elfenbein, D. (Ed.). (1995). *Living with Prozac and other selective sero-tonin-re-uptake inhibitors: Personal accounts of life on antidepressants.* New York: HarperCollins.

Elfenbein, D. (Ed.). (1996). *Living with tricyclic antidepressants: Personal accounts of life on Imipramine, Nortriptyline, Amitriptyline, and others.* New York: HarperCollins.

Elias, R. (1993). Crime wars forgotten. *Peace Review, 5*(1), 83–92.

Elias, R. (1997). A culture of violent solutions. In J. Turpin & L. R. Kurtz (Eds.), *The web of violence: From interpersonal to global.* Chicago: University of Chicago Press, pp. 117–148.

Engel, G. L. (1980). The clinical application of the biopsychsocial model. *American Journal of Psychiatry,* 137, 535–544.

Fechner, G. T. (1860). *Elemente der Psychophysik* [Elements of Psychophysics] (2 Vols.). Leipzig: Breitkopf and Hartel.

Feighner, J. P., Robbins, E., Guze, S. B., Woodruff, R. A., Winokur, G., & Munoz, R. (1972). Diagnostic criteria for use in psychiatric research. *Archives of General Psychiatry,* 26, 57–63.

Feinberg, I. (1987). Adolescence and mental illness [Letter to editor]. *Science,* 236, 507–508.

Fell, J. (1996, October). John William Miller and Nietzsche's Nihilism. *The Roy Wood Sellers Lecture,* Bucknell University, October 23, 1996.

Fell, J. (1997). Personal communication.

Finell, J. S. (1997). *Mind–body problems: Psychotherapy with psychosomatic disorders.* Northvale, NJ: Jason Aronson.

Fischer, C. T. (1978). Personality and assessment. In R. S. Valle & M. King (Eds). *Existential-phenomenological alternatives for psychology* (pp. 203–231). New York: Oxford University Press.

Fischman, J. (1987). Getting tough. *Psychology Today, 21*(12), 26–28.

Fisher, S., & Greenburg, R. G. (Eds.). (1989). *The limits of biological treatments for psychological distress.* Hillsdale, NJ: Lawrence Erlbaum Associates.

Frith, U. (1989). *Autism: Explaining the enigma.* Cambridge, MA: Blackwell.

Freud, S. (1905). Psychological treatment. *Standard Edition, Vol. III,* 283–302.

Freud, S. (1959). *Collected papers* (J. Riviere, Trans.). New York: Basic Books.

Freud, S. (1959). Mourning and melancholia. In S. Freud (J. Reviere, Trans.), *Collected papers.* New York: Basic Books.

Fulton, J. F. (1951). *Frontal lobotomy and affective behavior.* New York: Norton.

Gabbard, G. (1992). The big chill: The transition from residency to managed care nightmare. *Academic Psychiatry, 16,* 3.

Goldman-Rakic, P. S. (1993). Specification of higher cortical functions. *Journal of Head Trauma Rehabilitation, 8*(1), 13–23.

Greenblatt, D. J., & Shader, R. I. (1971). Meprobamate: A study of irrational drug use. *American Journal of Psychiatry, 127,* 1297–1303.

Grotstein, J. S. (1996). Orphans of the "real": I. Some modern and postmodern perspectives on neurobiological and psychosocial dimensions of psychosis and other primitive mental disorders. In J. C. Allen & D. T. Collins (Eds.), *Contemporary treatment of psychosis* (pp. 27–48). Northvale, NJ: Jason Aronson.

Group for the Advancement of Psychiatry. (1975). *Pharmacotherapy and psychotherapy: Paradoxes, problems, and progress.* New York: Mental Health Materials Center.

Healy, D. (1997). *The anti-depressant era.* Cambridge, MA: Harvard University Press.

Heidegger, M. (1962). *Being and time.* New York: Harper & Row. (Original work published 1927).

Heidegger, M. (1982). *The basic problems in phenomenology.* Bloomington: Indiana University Press.

Herman, H. J. M., & Kemper, H. J. G. (1993). *The dialogical self: Meaning as movement.* New York: Academic Press.

Horowitz, M. (1988). *Introduction to psychodynamics: A new synthesis.* New York: Basic Books.

Hutchings, N. (1992). Family violence. *Peace Review, 4*(3), 24–27.

Hutchinson, E. D. (1943). The phenomenon of insight in relation to religion. *Psychiatry, 6,* 347–387.

Illich, I. (1976). *Limits to medicine; Medical nemesis: The expropriation of health.* Baltimore: Penguin.

James, W. (1890). *Principles of psychology.* New York: Holt.

James, W. (1892). *Psychology: Briefer course.* New York: Holt.

Jaspers, K. (1975). *Reason and existence.* In S. Kaufman (Ed.) *Existentialism from Dostoevsky to Sartre.* New York: New American Library.

Jenkins, J. H. (1991). Anthropology, expressed emotion, and schizophrenia. *Ethos, 19,* 387–431.

Karasu, T. B. (1982). Psychotherapy and pharmacotherapy: Toward an integrative model. *American Journal of Psychiatry, 139,* 1102–1113.

Karno, M., Jenkins, J. H., de la Selva, A., Santana, F., Telles, C., Lopez, S., & Mintz, J. (1987). Expressed emotion and schizophrenic outcome among Mexican-American families. *Journal of Nervous and Mental Disease, 175*, 143–151.

Karp, D. (1996). *Speaking of sadness: Depression, disconnection, and the meaning of illness.* New York: Oxford University Press.

Kass, F., Charles, E., Walsh, T., & Barsa, J. (1983). Quality review of outpatient psychopharmacological practice with APA task force criteria. *American Journal of Psychiatry, 140*, 221–224.

Keen, E. (1975). *Primer in phenomenological psychology.* New York: Holt.

Keen, E. (1998). *Drugs, therapy, and professional power: Problems and pills.* Westport, CT: Praeger.

Kirk, S. A., & Kutchins, H. (1992). *The selling of DSM: The rhetoric of science in psychiatry.* New York: Aldine de Gruyter.

Kleinman, A. (1988). *Rethinking psychiatry: From cultural category to personal experience.* New York: The Free Press.

Knight, C. C. & Fischer, K. W. (1992). Learning to read words: Individual differences in developmental sequences. *Journal of Applied Developmental Psychology, 13*, 377–404.

Koehler, W. (1947). *Gestalt psychology.* New York: Liveright.

Krystal, H. (1982). Alexithymia and the effectiveness of psychoanalytic treatment. *International Journal of Psychoanalytic Psychotherapy, 9*, 353–378.

Kuhn, R. (1990). Contributions to discussion on the history of psychopharmacology at the Cambridge meeting on the history of physical treatments in psychiatry. *Journal of Psychopharmacology, 4*, 170.

Lafleur, F. J. (1964). *Descartes: Philosophical essays.* New York: Macmillan.

Laing, R. D. (1967). *The politics of experience.* New York: Pantheon.

Laing, R. D. (1971). *The politics of the family and other essays.* New York: Pantheon.

Leber, P. (1996). The role of the regulator in psychopharmacology. In D. Healy & D. Deign (Eds.), *Psychotropic drug development: Social, economic, and pharmacological aspects.* London: Chairman & Hall.

Leff, J. (1989). Family factors in schizophrenia. *Psychiatric Annals, 19*, 542–547.

Leifer, R. (1969). *In the name of mental health.* New York: Science House.

Lifton, R. J. (1997). Doubling: The Faustian bargain. In J. Turpin & L. R. Kurtz (Eds.), *The web of violence: From interpersonal to global.* (pp. 29–44). Chicago: University of Chicago Press.

Marcel, G. (1964). *Creative fidelity.* New York: Noonday Press.

Marshall, J. (1991). *Drug wars.* Forestville, CA: Cohan & Cohan.

Martins, C., de Lemos, A., & Bebbington, P. E. (1992). A Portuguese/Brazilian study of expressed emotion. *Social Psychiatry and Psychiatric Epidemiology, 27,* 22–27.

Matthiessen, P. (1989). *In the spirit of Crazy Horse.* New York: Simon & Schuster.

Merleau-Ponty, M. (1963). *The structure of behavior.* Boston: Beacon Press.

Merleau-Ponty, M. (1964). *The primacy of perception.* New York: Routledge & Kegan Paul.

Miller, J. W. (1983). *In defense of the psychological.* New York: Norton.

Morrison, R. (1995). *Ecological democracy.* Boston: South End Press.

Nemiah, J. C., & Sifneos, P. E. (1970). Affect and fantasy in patients with psychosomatic disorders. In O. W. Hill (Ed.), *Modern trends in psychosomatic medicine* (Vol. 2, pp. 26–34). London: Butterworth.

NIMH/NIH. (1985). Mood disorders: Pharmacologic prevention of recurrences. (Consensus Development Conference Statement). *American Journal of Psychiatry, 142,* 476–498.

Penick, E. C., Read, M. R., Lauchland, J. S., & Laybourne, P. C. (1991). Diagnosis-specific psychotherapy. In B. D. Beitman & G. K. Klerman, (Eds.), *Integrating pharmacotherapy and psychotherapy* (pp. 52–67). Washington, DC: American Psychiatric Press.

Pepper, S. C. (1942). *World hypotheses: A study in evidence.* Berkeley: University of California Press.

Piaget, J. (1955). *The language and thought of the child.* New York: Meridian.

Prado, C. G. (1992). *Descartes and Foucault: A contrastive introduction to philosophy.* Ottawa, Canada: University of Ottawa Press.

Preston, J., O'Neal, J. H., & Talaga, M. C. (1997). *Handbook of clinical pharmacology for therapists* (2nd ed.). Oakland, CA: New Harbinger.

Raskin, V. D. (1997). *When words are not enough: The women's prescription for depression and anxiety.* New York: Broadway Books.

Reiman, J. (1988). *The rich get richer and the poor get prison: Ideology, class, and criminal justice.* New York: Wiley.

Rogers, C. R. (1951). *Client-Centered Therapy.* Boston: Houghton, Mifflin.

Romanyshhyn, R. D. (1984). *Technology as symptom and dreams.* London: Routledge.

Ross, C. A., & Pam, A. (1995). *Pseudoscience in biological psychiatry: Blaming the body.* New York: Wiley.

Rush, B. (1962). *Medical inquiries and observations upon diseases of the mind.* New York: Hafner. (Original work published 1812).

Sacks, O. (1970). *The man who mistook his wife for his hat and other clinical tales.* New York: Simon & Shuster.

Said, E. (1979). *Orientalism.* New York: Vintage Books.

Sarbin, T. R., & Juhasz, J. B. (1982). The concept of mental illness. A historical perspective. In Al-Concept of· *Culture and Psychopathology* (pp. 71–110). Baltimore, MD: Univeristy Park Press.

Sarbin, T. R., & Keen, E. (1998). Non-traditional ways of classifying mental disorders. In H. S. Friedman (Ed.), *Encyclopedia of mental health* (pp. 461–473). San Diego: Academic Press.

Sarbin, T. R., & Mancuso, J. C. (1980). *Schizophrenia: Medical diagnosis or moral verdict?* New York: Pergamon.

Sartre, J.-P. (1949). *Being and having.* New York: Philosophical Library.

Sartre, J.-P. (1956). *Being and nothingness.* New York: Philosophical Library.

Schecter, S. (1982). *Women and male violence: The visions and struggles of the battered women's movement.* Boston: South End Press.

Schrag, C. O. (1997). *The self after postmodernity.* New Haven, CT: Yale University Press.

Scull, A. (1972). Social control and the amplification of deviance. In R. A. Scott & J. D. Douglas (Eds.), *Theoretical perspectives on deviance* (pp. 282–314). New York: Basic Books.

Scull, A. (1985). Deinstitutionalization and public policy. *Social Science and Medicine, 20,* 545–552.

Scull, A. (1987). Desperate remedies: A Gothic tale of madness and modern medicine. *Psychological Medicine, 17,* 561–577.

Scull, A. (1989). *Social order/mental disorder. Anglo-American psychiatry in historical perspective.* Berkeley: University of California Press.

Shephard, P. (1982). *Nature and madness.* San Francisco: Sierra Club Books.

Shutts, D. (1989). *Lobotomy: Resort to the knife.* New York: Van Nostrand.

Smith, M. B. (1999). Political psychology and peace: A half century perspective. Peace and conflict: *Journal of Peace Psychology, 5,* 1–16.

Sorell, T. (1987). *Descartes.* New York: Oxford University Press.

Sturm, D. (1998). *Solidarity and suffering; Toward a politics of relationality.* Albany: State University of New York Press.

Sullivan, H. S. (1940). *Conceptions of modern psychiatry.* New York: Norton.

Sullivan, H. S. (1962). *Schizophrenia as a human process.* New York: Norton.

Szasz, T. S. (1961). *The myth of mental illness: Foundations of a theory of personal conduct.* New York: Hoeber/Harper.

Szasz, T. S. (1987). *Insanity: The idea and its consequences.* New York: Wiley.

Thorndike, E. (1903). *Educational psychology.* New York: Lemke & Buechner.

Tolman, E. C. (1932). *Purposive behavior in animals and men.* New York: Century.

Torrey, E. F. (1988). *Surviving schizophrenia: A family manual.* New York: Harper & Row.

Valenstein, E. S. (1986). *Great and desperate cures: The rise and decline of psychosurgery and other radical treatments for mental illness.* New York: Basic Books.

Valenstein, E. S. (1998). *Blaming the brain: The truth about drugs and mental health.* New York: The Free Press.

Valle, R. S. & King, M. (1978). *Existential-phenomenological alternatives for psychology.* New York: Oxford University Press.

Valle, R. S., & von Eckartsberg, R. (1981). *Metaphors of consciousness.* New York: Plenum.

Voss, S. (Ed.). (1993). *Essays on the philosophy and science of Rene Descartes.* New York: Oxford University Press.

Watson, J. B. (1924). *Behaviorism.* Chicago: University of Chicago Press.

Watson, R. A. (1987). *The breakdown of Cartesian metaphysics.* Atlantic Highlands, NJ: Humanities Press International.

Wolpe, J. (1982). *The practice of behavior therapy* (3rd ed.). New York: Pergamon.

Wortis, J. (1955). Physiological treatment. *American Journal of Psychiatry, 112,* 515–518.

Wortis, J. (1965). Psychopharmacology and physiological treatment. *American Journal of Psychiatry, 121,* 648.

Wright, J. & Sheley, J. (1991). Teenage violence and the urban underclass. *Peace Review 4*(3), 32–35.

Index

Ernest Keen is Professor of Psychology at Bucknell University. He is the author of four earlier books, including *Drugs, Therapy, and Professional Power* (Praeger, 1998).